FOOTBALL BIOGRAPHIES FOR KIDS

★ ★ ☆

FOOTBALL BIOGRAPHIES

—— FOR KIDS ——

THE GREATEST NFL PLAYERS FROM THE 1960S TO TODAY

☆ ☆ ☆

DAVID HALPRIN

*Illustrations by
Monika Wiśniewska*

callisto
publishing
an imprint of Sourcebooks

Copyright © 2022 by Callisto Publishing LLC
Cover and internal design © 2022 by Callisto Publishing LLC
Illustrations © 2022 Monika Wiśniewska
Author photo courtesy of Jan Halprin
Series Designer: Eric Pratt
Interior and Cover Designer: Irene Vandervoort
Art Producer: Megan Baggott
Editor: Julia Maguire
Production Editor: Nora Milman
Production Manager: David Zapanta

Published by Callisto Publishing LLC C/O Sourcebooks LLC
P.O. Box 4410, Naperville, Illinois 60567-4410
(630) 961-3900
callistopublishing.com

Printed in the United States of America
VP 2

This one is for my dad, Ed Halprin. He taught me everything I needed to know to make my way in this world. He served his country as an Air Force officer, and he served his family in every way possible. We love you, POP.

CONTENTS

INTRODUCTION

By picking up this book, you have declared yourself a football fan. Thank you so much for joining us, the millions of National Football League (NFL) fans all around the world.

I have been covering NFL football for sixteen years. I'm lucky enough to cover my favorite team, the Dallas Cowboys, as a sportswriter at Blogging The Boys, a Cowboys site that I founded and edit. But before I started writing about the NFL, I was just a fan, like you. From the time I was six years old, I loved football.

You must know what that feels like—how exciting it is to follow the teams each week, to track the players and learn their stats. You want to know everything you can about the sport, where it started, and where it's headed.

How do players make it to the NFL? What were their failures and triumphs along the way? Where did they begin? When did they stop playing and who is still going strong? Can anyone definitively be called the greatest?

One of the toughest things is determining what exactly makes a player great. Is it their strong arm? How fast they can run? Maybe it's their ability to be a leader. Through eleven different positions and one coach, I highlight how these players rose to the top. You'll probably recognize many names, but there may be a few you won't.

One thing all the featured players have in common is their dedication to the game and the way they lived their lives off the field. Some players who had incredible stats had some trouble off the field, and as a result, they didn't make the cut. But there are countless deserving players to choose from, all with incredible stories. Unfortunately, this book just isn't long enough to include everybody.

But if you could assemble the perfect team, how would you do it? You could rely just on statistics, though those don't always tell the whole story. Some players have one perfect game or a terrific season, but then have their career cut short by injury. Some positions never get the glory, but teams couldn't win games without them. You have to look at the whole playing field.

This book covers players from 1960 and beyond, mostly people who played since the Super Bowl was created in 1967. There are legends covered here, but our focus is on the modern era of football. It has changed so much since the NFL formed in the 1920s. At the time, college football was much more popular, and players had to work another job in the off-season to make enough money to live. Now contracts are sky high!

But the league had to evolve to get there. It made smart decisions to get broadcast, first on radio and then television. It evened the playing field by implementing the draft and salary caps. Teams can't just buy their way to a championship, and all teams are competitive. So now, every season is a clean slate for teams and their fans. Next year could be your team's year!

I've spent a lifetime watching NFL football. Maybe you'll spend yours watching, too. Or maybe you'll work in the NFL. There are all kinds of jobs, not just players and coaches, but also the people who work in the front office and the people who sell tickets, do promotions, and look out for the team's needs. There are media people like me who cover the league, or you could be a referee. But of course, you can also just be a fan!

It's a thrilling sport to watch and a great one to learn about. Let this book open a door to discovering more about football and the NFL. Maybe you'll want to know even more about one of these players. Do your own research and learn everything you can. But first, it's time for kickoff, and we've got a lot to cover before that final whistle blows.

Let's go!

IMPORTANT STAT ACRONYMS

1ST DN (first downs): The number of times that a player got a first down for his team in his career

50+ FG MADE (50-or-more-yard field goal made): The number of times a player has successfully kicked a field goal that was 50 yards or longer

AVG (average): The average yards gained on a completion thrown by a player in his career

AVG RUSH (average yards per rush): The average yards per rushing attempt in a career

CATCH % (catch percentage): The percentage of catches a player made based on how many passes were thrown to them (which is called a target), on a scale of 0 percent to 100 percent, with the higher the percentage the better

COMP (completions): The number of successful throws and catches by an eligible receiver

FF (forced fumbles): The number of times a player causes a fumble in his career

FG ATT (field goal attempts): The number of times in a career that a player attempts to kick a field goal

FG MADE (field goals made): The number of times in a career that a player kicks a successful field goal

FG% (field goal percentage): The percentage is the number of times that a player made a field goal out of all of their attempts, on a scale of 0 percent to 100 percent, with the higher the percentage the better

FR (fumble recoveries): The number of times a player recovers a fumble in his career

FUMBLES: The number of fumbles a player had in his career

G (games played): All the games the player had at least one play on offense, defense, or special teams

G STARTED (games started): All the games the player started in his career

INT (interceptions): The number of interceptions made in a player's career

INT THROWN (interceptions thrown): The total number of interceptions (a forward pass is caught by the defense, resulting in a turnover) thrown by a player in his career

KO (kickoffs): The number of times a player has kicked off for their team

KR TD (kick return touchdowns): The total number of touchdowns a player has scored returning kicks in his career

KR YDS (kick return yards): The total number of yards a player has gained returning kicks in his career

L (losses): The number of times a head coach's team lost a game

PASS ATT (pass attempts): The number of passes thrown by a player in his career

PASS TD (passing touchdowns): The total number of pass completions that resulted in a touchdown for the passer

PASS YDS (passing yards): The total number of yards gained on completions thrown by a player

PCT (percentage): The percentage of passes thrown by a player that were completed, on a scale of 0 percent to 100 percent, with the higher the percentage the better (for example, if a player threw ten passes and completed seven of them, his PCT would be 70 percent)

PLAYOFF G (playoff games): The number of games in which a head coach or player participated

PLAYOFF INT (playoff interceptions): The number of interceptions a player made in the playoffs

PLAYOFF SACKS: The number of sacks a player made in the playoffs

PLAYOFF TD (playoff touchdowns): The number of touchdowns a player scored in the playoffs

PLAYOFF W (playoff wins): The number of playoff games a head coach participated in and won

PLAYOFF WIN % (playoff win percentage): Out of all the games a head coach participated in during the play-offs, the number of times he won on a scale of 0 percent to 100 percent, with the higher the percentage the better

PR TD (punt return touchdowns): The total number of touchdowns a player has scored returning punts in his career

PR YDS (punt return yards): The total number of yards a player has gained returning punts in his career

QB RATE (quarterback rating): This number comes from a formula that takes into account different stats for a quarterback in his career and is used to compare one quarterback to another, with the higher the number the better

REC (receptions): This is the number of times a player caught a forward pass in his career

REC TD (receiving touchdowns): The total number of touchdowns scored through receptions in a player's career

REC YDS (receiving yards): The total number of yards gained through receptions in a player's career

RUSH ATT (rushing attempts): This represents the total number of rushes (when an offensive player runs the ball) in a career for a player

RUSH TD (rushing touchdown): The total number of times a player ran the ball for a touchdown

RUSH YDS/G (rushing yards per game): How many rushing yards a player got on average in a game in his career

SACKS (sacks credited to a player on defense): Sacks occur when the offensive player who has the ball and is intending to pass (usually the quarterback) is tackled or forced out of bounds behind the line of scrimmage

SAFETY (caused a safety): A player is credited with causing a safety (worth two points) mainly when he tackles the offensive player with the ball in the offense's own end zone

TACKLES: The number of tackles in a player's career

TB% (touchback percentage): The percentage is the number of times that a player kicked off and the other team took a touchback instead of trying to run the kick back, on a scale of 0 percent to 100 percent, with the higher the percentage the better

W (wins): The number of times a head coach's team won a game

WIN% (win percentage): Out of all the games a head coach participated in, the number of times he won, on a scale of 0 percent to 100 percent, with the higher the percentage the better

XP ATT (extra point attempts): The number of times in a career that a player attempts to kick an extra point

XP MADE (extra points made): The number of times in a career that a player kicks a successful extra point

XP% (extra point percentage): The percentage is the number of times that a player made an extra point out of all of their attempts, on a scale of 0 percent to 100 percent, with the higher the percentage the better

YDS/G (yards per game): The average number of yards a player gained per game in their career

YDS/REC (yards per reception): The number of yards on average that a player gained per reception

FAST FACTS

Super Bowls are numbered in roman numerals to avoid confusion with the year the game takes place. For example, the 30th Super Bowl looks like Super Bowl XXX. This helps others avoid thinking that the game took place in 1930 (when it actually took place in 1996.)

TOM BRADY

QUARTERBACK

JERSEY NUMBER	12
HEIGHT | WEIGHT	6' 4" | 225 LBS
BORN	AUGUST 3, 1977
HOMETOWN	SAN MATEO, CALIFORNIA
ACTIVE YEARS	2000–PRESENT

CAREER STATS

(Through the 2021–2022 season)

G: 318	AVG: 7.5
PASS ATT: 11,317	PASS TD: 624
COMP: 7,263	INT (THROWN): 203
PCT: 64.18	QB RATE: 97.6
PASS YDS: 84,520	PLAYOFF G: 47

5X SUPER BOWL MVP

3X LEAGUE MVP

15X PRO BOWL

"I think sometimes in life the biggest challenges end up being the best things that happen in your life."

A NEW START

Imagine you had spent your whole life doing one thing, in one place, with most of the same people, year after year. Then you decide you want something new. You leave everything you know and start a new adventure in a new city with new people. That's what Tom Brady did in 2020 when he left the New England Patriots and started over with the Tampa Bay Buccaneers. In his first season there, Tampa Bay was doing well. The team made the playoffs but were only the fifth seed in the National Football Conference (NFC). Its playoff games were going to be away games, and it looked like a tough road for the team. But Brady was never the kind of player to back down from a challenge.

He went on to do what many believed would never happen. He led his Buccaneers to three wins in the play-offs to reach Super Bowl LV. He didn't stop there. In the title game, he faced the powerhouse Kansas City Chiefs, a team that many thought was the best in the NFL and would be unbeatable for a long time.

At the big game, he led his team to a 31–9 victory. He won another Super Bowl MVP award—his fifth! He did it without the great Bill Belichick, his longtime coach in New England. He shed his past and became a champ again. Throughout his career, he had been doubted many times, but he always worked hard, won, and won again. Now he had capped that off with another amazing season. He was truly the GOAT: the Greatest of All Time.

THE BRADY BUNCH

Thomas Edward Patrick Brady Jr. was born on August 3, 1977, in San Mateo, California. Growing up, Brady idolized a San Francisco 49ers quarterback named Joe Montana. He would go to games and watch from the stands hoping to learn from the master. He was even in the stands when Joe Montana threw his famous touchdown, now known simply as "The Catch," to Dwight Clark in the 1981 NFC Championship game.

The Bradys were a very close-knit family that loved sports and loved to compete. Even at a young age, Tom played flag football and was naturally the quarterback. He attended a youth camp in California where he learned about playing quarterback from future NFL quarterback Tony Graziani.

FROM BASEBALL TO FOOTBALL

Brady went to Junipero Serra High School, and like many famous athletes, he competed in baseball first. When he did join the football team, he didn't even start. That wasn't the last time that happened to him. But eventually, he became the starting quarterback, and soon, major colleges showed interest in his skills.

He made the decision to attend the University of Michigan on a football scholarship in 1995. Once again, Brady did not begin as a starter. He was behind Brian

Griese, the son of famous NFL legend Bob Griese, as well as several other players. It took a few years for Brady to get his chance. Finally, in his junior year, he not only started but excelled and won game after game. And when he graduated from Michigan in 1999, he set his sights on the NFL draft.

A TRUE MVP

As had happened before, Brady was initially overlooked in the 2000 draft. Six NFL teams took quarterbacks before Brady was chosen. Then, with the 199th pick, the New England Patriots chose him. But once again, Brady was a backup. Not even the first backup, but fourth string! He had been here before, and it was only a matter of time before he got his chance.

By the end of his rookie year, he was the first backup to the quarterback. In his second year, starter Drew Bledsoe suffered an injury late in the second game of the season. Brady replaced him. He started every game from then on and led the Patriots to the Super Bowl. They played the Los Angeles Rams, a team so good that the Patriots were widely expected to lose big. Instead, Brady led them to a 20–17 victory and received his first Super Bowl Most Valuable Player (MVP) trophy. He had done what he always did: overcome expectations and beat the odds.

And Brady just kept winning. Over his career, he won 243 regular-season games and thirty-five more in the playoffs. That's the best ever for a quarterback! In 2007, he led the Patriots to a perfect regular-season record of sixteen wins and no losses. He won the NFL MVP award in 2007, 2010, and 2017. He has seven Super Bowl wins for the 2001, 2003, 2004, 2014, 2016, 2018, and 2020 seasons. Players are still trying to beat records that he set.

THE GOAT

Tom Brady isn't the biggest, he isn't the fastest, and he doesn't have the most powerful throwing arm. All through his career, people found reasons not to expect much from him. But he worked harder than anybody, and every time, he proved them wrong. He was certain he would be a big success, even as he started in the NFL.

The owner of the Patriots, Robert Kraft, recalls meeting Brady for the first time after the team drafted him. "I still have the image of Tom Brady coming down the old Foxboro stadium steps with that pizza box under his arm, a skinny beanpole, and when he introduced himself to me and said, 'Hi, Mr. Kraft,' he was about to say who he was, but I said 'I know who you are, you're Tom Brady. You're our sixth-round draft choice,'" recalled Kraft. "And he looked me in the eye and said, 'I'm the best decision this organization has ever made.' It looks like he could be right." There's no doubt he was.

FAST FACTS

- The Montreal Expos drafted Brady in the eighteenth round as a catcher in the 1995 MLB draft, hoping he would play baseball instead of going to Michigan.

- Brady missed the 2008 season after a knee injury in the first game, and that was the only time in his NFL career he missed a game because of an injury.

- He was the oldest quarterback to ever win a Super Bowl and be named the MVP of the game at age of forty-three.

Runners-up

JOE MONTANA

Joe Montana was Tom Brady's idol. He was called "the GOAT" long before Brady came along. Montana led the San Francisco 49ers to four Super Bowl titles in the 1980s. He won the league MVP award twice and was the Super Bowl MVP three times. He also led the Kansas City Chiefs to the AFC Championship Game in the 1993 season. He was nicknamed "Joe Cool" because he was calm even when things were going badly.

PEYTON MANNING

Peyton Manning was the quarterback for two different teams that won the Super Bowl: the Indianapolis Colts in the 2006 season and the Denver Broncos in the 2015 season. He won five league MVP awards, more than any other player. He is part of the Manning QB Family that includes his father Archie Manning and younger brother, Eli Manning.

Legendary Great

JOHNNY UNITAS

Have you ever been picked as one of the last players on a team for a playground game? If so, don't worry. Even the best NFL quarterbacks can be overlooked at first. Take one of the greats, Johnny Unitas. He wasn't a first-round, third-round, or even seventh-round pick. He wasn't taken until the ninth round! On top of that, his first team got rid of him, and he had to start over with another team the next year.

None of that stopped Unitas. He went on to win the 1959, 1964, and 1967 NFL MVP awards. He helped the Baltimore Colts win three NFL titles, and he was part of the team that won the fifth Super Bowl. In 1979, he was voted into the Pro Football Hall of Fame and was given the nickname the "Golden Arm." Johnny Unitas may not have started with a lot of attention, but he ended his career as a legend.

Spotlight

EIGHT QUARTERBACKS WHO HAVE THROWN SEVEN TOUCHDOWNS IN ONE GAME

If you throw one touchdown in a game, you had a pretty good week. Throw four touchdowns? You are going to be on the highlight reels on ESPN. Throw seven touchdowns in one game? Then you'll join a very short list of just eight other quarterbacks.

Drew Brees did it for the Saints against the Giants in 2015. Others who did it:

Nick Foles (Eagles vs. Raiders, 2013)

Peyton Manning (Broncos vs. Ravens, 2013)

Joe Kapp (Vikings vs. Colts, 1969)

Y.A. Tittle (Giants vs. Washington, 1962)

George Blanda (Oilers vs. Titans, 1961)

Adrian Burk (Eagles vs. Washington, 1954)

Sid Luckman (Bears vs. Giants, 1943)

Beating the Odds

KURT WARNER

Kurt Warner is one of the greatest undrafted players ever. He wasn't drafted by any team in the 1994 draft. (Are you starting to see a theme for some of the greatest players in the game?) He was stocking shelves at a grocery store for $5.50 an hour while waiting for his chance to arrive.

He played in the Arena Football League and in NFL Europe until finally, the Los Angeles Rams put him on the team in 1998 as a backup. After an injury to the starter in 1999, Warner was thrust into the starting quarterback role for the Rams. He led the team to the big prize and won the Super Bowl. He was named MVP, and the Rams offense was the reason the team was nicknamed "The Greatest Show on Turf." The team played its home games on artificial turf, and they scored a lot of points doing it.

Warner played for twelve NFL seasons and was in two more Super Bowls, with the Rams and then with the Arizona Cardinals. His whole career was a longshot, but he beat the odds.

Kurt Warner

WALTER PAYTON

RUNNING BACK

JERSEY NUMBER	34
HEIGHT | WEIGHT	5' 10" | 200 LBS
BORN	JULY 25, 1954
HOMETOWN	COLUMBIA, MISSISSIPPI
ACTIVE YEARS	1975–1987

CAREER STATS

G: 190	REC YDS: 4,538
RUSH ATT: 3,838	REC TD: 15
YDS: 16,726	RUSH YDS/G: 88
RUSH TD: 110	PASS TD: 8
REC: 492	KR YDS: 539

5X FIRST-TEAM ALL-PRO

NFL MVP 1977

9X PRO BOWL

"All people, regardless of whether they are athletes or not, should treat people the way they want to be treated."

MAN OF THE YEAR

There are many ways to be great, and Walter Payton was all of them. On the field, he was as good as anyone. Off the field, he was even better. It's easy to say that, but there is proof in this case. It's not in the runs, or the catches, or the touchdowns, or the records, or even the Super Bowl win. All of that is important, but first, let's focus on the year 1999.

From 1970 to 1999, the NFL handed out the NFL Man of the Year award to a player who was excellent on and off the field. Someone who helped others and worked with charities. It's a very big deal. Past winners include Peyton Manning, Larry Fitzgerald, and Russell Wilson, just to name a few.

In 1999, the NFL made a change. It would no longer hand out the NFL Man of the Year Award but would instead award the Walter Payton NFL Man of the Year Award. That is how much everyone thought of Walter Payton. They not only thought of him as a great football player but as a great human being. It was a fitting honor for Payton, who had previously won the award in 1977. It's tough to think of a bigger honor than having this award named after you.

LITTLE DRUMMER BOY

When Payton was young, he didn't even want to be a football player. He was more interested in activities like music and the Boy Scouts. He was a drummer and played in bands, including the one at his school. He sang in the church choir.

He grew up in the shadow of his older brother, Eddie, who was a star athlete in high school. One reason why Walter didn't play football was because he didn't want to compete against his brother and preferred to stick to his music. Before Walter even tried football in high school, he ran track.

SWEETNESS

Payton's high school football coach talked him into trying football, even though his older brother was a star player and Walter didn't want to compete with him. But the first time they gave him the ball in a game, he ran sixty-five yards for a touchdown. From then on, he played football and basketball, ran track, and still kept drumming in the band.

When it came time for college, Payton didn't choose a major football school. He went to Jackson State University, just like his brother. He joined the team, but he was there for more than football, majoring in education and wanting to help people who are deaf. He was always thinking of others.

Right before the 1975 draft, at a college football all-star game, he earned the nickname "Sweetness" from the other players. It was said that the nickname was given to him for his "sweet" moves on the field and his "sweet" personality off of it. The nickname stuck with him for the rest of his life.

A POWERFUL PLAYER

The Chicago Bears picked Payton to be one of their running backs during the draft. In his second year with the Bears, he took over the running back duties full-time. Payton wasn't just a runner. He was a top pass catcher, not to mention a great blocker. Jack Youngblood, a player on another team, can't forget a time he was blocked by Payton. "'I remember a block he threw on me once and I thought he opened a hole in my [chest], he hit me so hard. I said, 'Walter, what are you doing?' He said, 'You were in the way.'"

There was nothing Payton couldn't do on the football field. And he did it all with force and power. He might have been kind and sweet off the field, but he was a physical player who never avoided contact. Instead of tacklers punishing him with hits, he punished the tacklers.

But even on the field, he showed how much he cared about others and wanted to make sure everyone got credit. After scoring a touchdown, he would sometimes hand the ball to his offensive linemen saying, "they're the ones who do all the work."

His strength and workouts were also famed among other members of the league. Before each season started, he would run up a steep hill near his home. He would invite other athletes to join him, but they would tire out after a few runs. It was said Payton would run it twenty times a day.

All that work paid off. He missed only one game due to an injury throughout his career. That is unheard of for a running back, one of the toughest, most injury-prone positions in the NFL. And this went on for thirteen seasons!

In 1985, everything came together for Payton and the Bears. They had a 15–1 record going into the playoffs. They went on to the Super Bowl and won 46–10 over the New England Patriots.

RECORDS AND RESPECT

By the time he retired in 1987, Payton had rewritten the record book. He held the title for most rushing yards (16,276) until Emmitt Smith broke it in 2002. He also set the record for most rushing yards in a game (275), most career rushing touchdowns (110), and most combined rushing and receiving yards (21,264). Those records have been broken, but in his time, no one could catch Payton.

Mike Ditka, Payton's coach and himself a former football great, said of Walter that he was "the very best football player I've ever seen, period, at any position."

Payton died from liver disease in 1999, but he left behind a legacy of respect and admiration from fans and his fellow players. That is why the NFL Man of the Year Award bears his name. On and off the field, no one was better.

FAST FACTS

- Walter Payton threw eight touchdown passes in his career. That's the most by a non-quarterback in the modern game.

- Walter Payton was so talented at the game of football that he was sometimes the kicker for his college team in addition to a running back.

- When Payton set a then-record of 275 rushing yards in one game against the Vikings in 1977, he was sick with the flu.

Runners-up

BARRY SANDERS

Barry Sanders only played ten seasons for the Detroit Lions but made the most of them. Sanders was known for amazing runs that seemed like something out of a video game. He finished with 15,269 rushing yards, good for fourth place in the NFL. In 1997, he topped 2,000 yards (2,053), one of only eight NFL running backs to ever do that.

EMMITT SMITH

Emmitt Smith is the NFL's all-time leading rusher in yards, with 18,355 yards, most of them with the Dallas Cowboys. He is also the leader in rushing touchdowns, with 164. He won three Super Bowls with the Cowboys and was the MVP of Super Bowl XXVIII.

LaDAINIAN TOMLINSON

LaDainian Tomlinson deserves a lot more attention than he gets. For eleven seasons, he was a touchdown machine for the San Diego Chargers, scoring 162 touchdowns, behind Jerry Rice and Emmitt Smith. He is seventh all time in rushing yards and holds the single-season record for touchdowns (31), winning the MVP award and the Walter Payton NFL Man of the Year award that same year (2006).

Legendary Great

JIM THORPE

Jim Thorpe is one of the early heroes in sports. He was a Native American member of the Sac and Fox Nation. His Sac and Fox name was Wa-Tho-Huck, which means "Bright Path."

He won gold medals in the pentathlon and decathlon in the 1912 Olympics and then went on to be a star football player in college. He also played baseball and lacrosse, and he even won a championship in ballroom dancing!

Thorpe could play just about any sport. He played pro baseball in the major leagues and travelled around with a basketball team. He also played football for the Canton Bulldogs. They were one of the original teams to form the NFL. With Thorpe, Canton won titles in 1916, 1917, and 1919. At one time, he even coached the team.

Thorpe was a rare all-around player. He ran with power and speed, and he could catch as well as kick field goals and punt. He could play any sport at the highest level. It's no wonder he has been called "The World's Greatest Athlete."

Jim Thorpe

POWER BACK NICKNAMES

What do you get when you mix the strength and attitude of a fullback with the running skills of a halfback? You get the power back! These players draw a following for their physical play as well as their interesting nicknames. That's right. The power backs have had some of the very best nicknames in the NFL. One of the most recent is "Beast Mode," for Marshawn Lynch because he would just run over people instead of going around them. More great nicknames include:

Craig "Ironhead" Heyward: From 1988 to 1998, Heyward played for five different teams. In 1995 he ran 1,083 yards for the Atlanta Falcons. At a reported weight of about 265 pounds, he was huge.

Christian Okoye, "The Nigerian Nightmare": From 1987 to 1992, a power back was scaring defenses around the NFL. Born in Nigeria, Okoye was 250 pounds of solid muscle while standing 6' 1". He led the NFL in rushing yards for 1989 (1,480) and had a superhero nickname, "The Nigerian Nightmare."

Jerome "The Bus" Bettis: Need a ride? Hop on "The Bus." Bettis got his nickname in college, when it was said players looked like people going for a ride on the bus while trying to tackle him. Bettis played from 1993 to 2005 and won a Super Bowl. He is one of the best power backs to ever play the game.

JIM BROWN

FULLBACK

JERSEY NUMBER 32
HEIGHT | WEIGHT 6' 2" | 232 LBS
BORN FEBRUARY 17, 1936
HOMETOWN SAINT SIMONS ISLAND, GEORGIA
ACTIVE YEARS 1957–1965

CAREER STATS

G: 118

RUSH ATT: 2,359

RUSH YDS: 12,312

AVG RUSH: 5.2

RUSH TD: 106

RUSH YDS/G: 104.3

REC: 262

REC YDS: 2,499

YDS/REC: 9.5

REC TD: 20

8X FIRST-TEAM ALL-PRO

3X LEAGUE MVP

9X PRO BOWL

"I wanted to help others and I credit those who helped me."

A MIND FOR DETAILS

Jim Brown appears on many lists as the best fullback ever. That may be true, but you could also make the case that he is the best football *player* ever.

Brown was very big for a running back in his day. Even today, he would be considered on the large end of the scale. But he could also run and had incredible balance. He was a new kind of player that would have fit right into today's NFL, where the players are bigger and faster.

He played the fullback position in the NFL. Back in 1960, after a few years in the NFL, Brown wrote a short article for *Sports Illustrated* magazine that was titled "How I Play Fullback." He said, "At the beginning of a play, I literally use a three-point stance. My right toe is on a line a bit behind the left heel. My head is up, I am balanced lightly by my right fingertips, and I am in a position, coming out of the crouch, to look for my opening and blockers."

Brown made sure he learned every detail of how to best play the game. He studied it, and then he made sure to use his knowledge of the game when he played. He was prepared for his job and was putting in the work to be a champion. Sure, Brown had amazing skill and size, but he used his brain, too.

STARTING YOUNG

Brown was born in Georgia in 1936 and was a star athlete at a young age. His father left the family early in Jim's life, and his mother moved to New York to find work. Brown was raised at that time by his great-grandmother. He moved to New York when he was eight years old to live with his mother. He started playing sports, including football, as a way to fit in at his new home.

JACK OF ALL TRADES

In high school, Brown's average yards per carry as a running back was 14.9, an astounding number. He also averaged more than thirty-eight points per game in basketball at his high school.

He played football, baseball, basketball, and lacrosse and ran track at Syracuse University. There, he gained national fame as a football player and as one of the best lacrosse players in the country. His versatility made him a rare athlete. In his senior year at Syracuse, Brown was voted an All-American. He came in fifth for the Heisman Trophy. In Brown's final game for Syracuse, against Colgate, he led his team to a 61–7 win. He ran for 197 yards, scored six touchdowns, and kicked seven extra points. He also led the lacrosse team to an undefeated 10–0 season.

RUSHING TO THE PROS

In 1957, the Cleveland Browns picked Brown (the perfect fit!) in the NFL draft. The rest of the league had no idea what was coming. In only his ninth professional game, Brown ran for 237 yards, setting a record that no first-year player would break for forty years.

By his second season, Brown was setting the record for most rushing yards in a season. And he never looked back. He won the MVP award three times. He was picked for the Pro Bowl all of his nine years in the NFL. He was a First-Team All-Pro eight times. He was simply the most dominant force the NFL had ever seen.

He was a mix of power, speed, and balance. He would take on tacklers and deliver as much of a hit on them as they planned to do to him. It was difficult for just one player to tackle him. Defenses were forced to plan for Brown on every play. Even when they did that, it was still nearly impossible for them to stop him.

MORE THAN FOOTBALL

When he retired, Brown held every important record for running backs: most yards in a season (1,863), career rushing yards (12,312), and touchdowns (106). He is the only running back to average more than one hundred yards per game (104.3). In 1964, Brown won the biggest prize in a team sport when his Cleveland Browns won the NFL Championship. At this point, you might think that was the best part of his life. But Brown's fame didn't fade after he retired. He just started a whole new career.

He became an actor and appeared in dozens of films and television shows, including *The Dirty Dozen*. He also became an activist, fighting for the rights of people. Brown was a voice for change. He helped set up businesses, athletic clubs, and other programs for youths to help improve their lives. His programs helped people whose lives had gone in the wrong direction get back to doing good in their own communities.

Brown was a gifted football player, but he didn't just rest on his physical ability. He used his mind, too. He thought about things, studied, then put his knowledge into action. Whether on the football field or out in the world, he always worked to do his best. And when he failed or got off course, he didn't walk away, but rather tried to do better.

FAST FACTS

- Jim Brown is not just in the Pro Football Hall of Fame, but also in the College Football Hall of Fame and the Lacrosse Hall of Fame.

- He could have gone to the 1956 Olympics as a decathlete, but instead, Jim Brown decided to focus his efforts on football.

- Brown was born on the same date, February 17, as another sports all-time legend, basketball's Michael Jordan.

Runners-up

LARRY CSONKA

Like Jim Brown, Larry Csonka went to college at Syracuse University. He was part of the Miami Dolphins' perfect 17–0 season in 1972. He won two Super Bowls with the team and was the MVP in one of them. To this day, forty years later, he is still the Dolphins' all-time leading rusher (6,737). He went to five Pro Bowls and was First-Team All-Pro three times.

FRANCO HARRIS

Franco Harris won four Super Bowls with the Pittsburgh Steelers. He was named the MVP of Super Bowl IX. He was picked for nine Pro Bowls and won the Offensive Rookie of the Year award in 1972. He is best remembered for the "Immaculate Reception." That is one of the most famous NFL plays ever. He caught a tipped pass and ran for a touchdown in the final seconds to win a playoff game.

MIKE ALSTOTT

Mike Alstott is one of the last great fullbacks who also ran the ball. He played eleven seasons for the Tampa Bay Buccaneers. He won a Super Bowl, went to six Pro Bowls, and was First-Team All-Pro three times. In addition to being able to run the ball, Alstott could also catch passes and deliver huge blocks.

MARION MOTLEY

Marion Motley played for nine years in the All-American Football Conference (AAFC) and NFL (1946–1953 and 1955). Eight of those nine years were for the Cleveland Browns. He became one of the first Black players in the modern era of pro football. This happened just before Jackie Robinson did the same thing in major league baseball.

The Browns were part of the All-American Football Conference (AAFC), a rival league to the NFL. With Motley, they won that league's first four titles. In 1950, the Browns joined the NFL, and Motley continued to play for the team.

He is thought of as one of the most powerful runners the game's followers have ever seen. He also played linebacker on defense in his early years. In 1950, he led the NFL in rushing yards, and his team won the NFL title. He averaged an incredible 5.7 yards per rushing attempt. That is still the record for running backs.

Motley has been called the best fullback ever, and there are some who believe he was among the best football players ever.

WHAT IS THE DIFFERENCE BETWEEN A FULLBACK AND A HALFBACK?

Fullbacks and halfbacks are part of a position group called running backs. Over the history of the NFL, the roles of these two positions have changed. Even the term "halfback" has kind of gone away in the NFL today. There are still fullbacks, but they are not like they used to be. Sometimes players were a mixture of fullback and halfback, like the power backs we talked about in the previous chapter.

Fullbacks are mostly thought of as bigger, stronger backs. Long ago, their role was to run on the inside of the offensive line—meaning between the two offensive tackles. They were also supposed to block, either for the halfback or on a pass play. Sometimes, they caught passes, too.

The halfbacks were mostly smaller, quicker backs. They would run to the outside and go out in pass patterns to catch the ball. They also lined up in different places. Offenses sometimes lined up in something called an "I formation." In that formation, the fullback was three or four yards behind the line of scrimmage, and the halfback was behind him, seven yards or so from the line of scrimmage.

As time went on, some teams started using only one back on offense. That back had to be able to run inside and outside and also catch passes. They ended up just calling him a running back instead of a halfback. The fullback became a position that mainly blocked for the running back, and the running back caught passes.

In today's football, many teams don't even have a fullback. Those that do use them as blockers, and not even on every play. Sometimes, if a team is just trying to get a yard or two on a play, they may hand the ball to a fullback. But they mostly block. The running backs do almost all of the work when it comes to running the ball.

JERRY RICE

WIDE RECEIVER

JERSEY NUMBER	80
HEIGHT | WEIGHT	6' 2" | 200 LBS
BORN	OCTOBER 13, 1962
HOMETOWN	CRAWFORD, MISSISSIPPI
ACTIVE YEARS	1985–2004

CAREER STATS

G: 303	YDS/G: 75.6
REC: 1,549	PLAYOFF G: 29
REC YDS: 22,895	PLAYOFF TD: 22
REC TD: 197	FUMBLES: 27
YDS/REC: 14.8	RUSH TD: 10

3X SUPER BOWL CHAMP (SB 23 MVP)

10X FIRST-TEAM ALL-PRO

13X PRO BOWL

"I was determined to be the best football player I could be on the football field, and I think I was able to accomplish that through hard work."

BUILT WITH BRICKS

When you think of the greatest wide receiver of all time, you might not think of bricks. Why would you? The best receiver ever surely grew up catching footballs.

But bricks are an important part of the Jerry Rice story. He built his work ethic with bricks. He built his strong hands with bricks. You could say he built a Hall of Fame career on bricks. Jerry Rice is proof that if you can catch a brick, you can catch a football.

RUNNING WITH THE HORSES

Rice's father was a brick mason, and sometimes he would bring his sons with him to work. That is where Jerry and his brother started their unique way of training for football, even though they didn't know that it would pay off in football skills later. Jerry described it this way: " . . . during the summer, my father would take me to work with him . . . My brother and I, we had developed this technique where you throw the bricks up, they were separated, and I was snatching them in the air. So, the myth about me learning to catch footballs from catching bricks, that's where it came from."

Rice was born in Mississippi in 1962, one of eight children. Growing up, Rice was never far away from hard work. Besides catching bricks, he also caught horses that had gotten free by running after them, sometimes for up to an hour. Athletic training and hard work went hand in hand for Rice as a young man.

A HIGH SCHOOL STAR

Rice didn't take up football until he was in high school. One day, a teacher caught him cutting class, but Rice ran away from him very quickly. The teacher had Rice pay the price for skipping, but also told the football coach how fast Rice ran. Before long, Rice was playing football. Once he did, it shaped his path for the rest of his life.

All that natural training with his family had paid off. Almost immediately, he started getting attention from colleges for his football skills. He chose Mississippi Valley State and became a star. He set records for catches in a season (112) and also for yards in a season (1,845). Even though he played at a school in a smaller division of college football, he was ninth in the Heisman Trophy voting.

FROM MISSISSIPPI TO SAN FRANCISCO

The San Francisco 49ers chose Rice in the 1985 NFL Draft with the sixteenth pick. In his rookie season, he won an Offensive Rookie of the Year award. By the next year, he was a big star, leading the entire league in yards with 1,570.

From there, Rice set record after record and won award after award—too many to even name them here! He won three Super Bowl titles with the 49ers. But Super Bowl XXIII was perhaps the greatest moment of Rice's entire career.

In that game against the Cincinnati Bengals, he caught eleven passes for 215 yards and was named the MVP. That number of receiving yards is still a record for Super Bowls that stands today, more than thirty years later! He also holds the record for most catches in Super Bowls (33) and most receiving yards in Super Bowls (589). When it mattered most, Jerry Rice played his best.

The owner of the 49ers, Edward DeBartolo Jr., once said of Rice: "I've never seen a player more driven or willing to work harder to become the greatest of all time. His perfectionism was evident in everything he did, in the way he carried himself both on and off the field."

THE REWARDS OF HARD WORK

Even after playing for twenty seasons, Jerry Rice was rarely injured. All those days working hard and catching bricks in his youth had formed one of the best NFL players to play the game of football. And the proof is in his lasting legacy. More than fifteen years after he last played, he still holds some of the most important records in the game. He has the most catches ever (1,549), the most receiving yards ever (22,895), and the most touchdowns ever (208). He still holds more than thirty-eight records.

Rice is more proof that you don't have to be the biggest or fastest in the game, but by hard work, you can become one of the best. Maybe catching bricks isn't the way everybody should go about it, but it worked for Rice. It took him to the very top. Good thing he laid a brick floor to rest all those awards on.

FAST FACTS

- The NFL declared Jerry Rice the best football player ever in its series *The Top 100: NFL's Greatest Players*. He and Jim Brown are regularly listed as the two best in the game.

- In season two of the show *Dancing with the Stars*, Jerry Rice came in second place.

- Jerry Rice loves to play golf, and after he retired from football, he tried to become a pro golfer.

Runners-up

RANDY MOSS

Randy Moss played from 1998 to 2012 and was the receiving touchdown leader in a season five different times. His ability to jump over the defensive players and catch the ball was his most impressive skill. He was the Offensive Rookie of the Year (1998) and was on the First-Team All-Pro squad four times. He caught 982 passes for 15,292 yards.

TERRELL OWENS

Terrell Owens played for five different teams from 1996 to 2010, roughly the same time as Moss. He led the league in receiving touchdowns three times and went to six Pro Bowls. He was once a teammate of Jerry Rice in San Francisco. He finished with 1,078 catches and 15,934 receiving yards. His big, over-the-top personality also made him a memorable part of the NFL.

LARRY FITZGERALD JR.

Larry Fitzgerald Jr. finished a seventeen-year career in 2020, all for the Arizona Cardinals. He went to eleven Pro Bowls and is second in all-time receiving yards (17,492) and career catches (1,432). He won the Walter Payton NFL Man of the Year Award in 2016. His quiet personality and ability to do his job at such a high level make him an unforgettable wide receiver.

Legendary Great

DON HUTSON

Back in the 1930s and '40s, there was a wide receiver who changed the game. His name was Don Hutson. He is called the first real modern receiver and was the kind of player who made passing the ball, instead of running it, a real possibility for the offense. He played his whole career for the Green Bay Packers and won three championships (1936, '39, and '44).

Before Hutson, passing was not the way offenses moved the ball. He showed that it could be the best way to win. The first catch he ever made in the NFL went for eighty-three yards and a touchdown. He led the NFL in receiving touchdowns nine out of his eleven years in the game. During the 1941 season, he caught fifty-eight passes, which was the first time anybody had ever caught more than fifty in a season.

Hutson also had another trick to his game. He was the kicker for many seasons, scoring 172 extra points and seven field goals.

Spotlight

BEST SINGLE-SEASON RECEIVING CORPS

2000 Rams' Torry Holt, Isaac Bruce, Az-Zahir Hakim, Marshall Faulk, and Ricky Proehl

Remember Kurt Warner and "The Greatest Show on Turf"? Even with one of the best quarterbacks, the receivers for the Los Angeles Rams' 2000 season are considered one of the best groups ever. They caught a whopping 253 passes for 4,281 yards. And they scored, too—a lot—unless you don't think twenty-three touchdowns is a lot.

Isaac Bruce

Isaac Bruce is a Hall of Fame player who had 1,471 yards that season. He was only topped by the other main receiver, Torry Holt, with 1,635 yards. Bruce and Holt were among the best receivers in the NFL, and they were on the same team!

Az-Zahir Hakim added 734 yards while Ricky Proehl chipped in 441 yards. And don't forget running back Marshall Faulk and his amazing 830 yards receiving.

The offense was a points machine. There was nothing they couldn't do—go long, go short, or make big plays after the catch. They led the league in total passing yards (5,492) and passing touchdowns (37) on their way to sixty-three total offensive touchdowns for the team. It was truly a passing attack for the ages. They made NFL defenses look silly trying to cover all that firepower.

TONY GONZALEZ

TIGHT END

JERSEY NUMBER	88
HEIGHT | WEIGHT	6' 5" | 247 LBS
BORN	FEBRUARY 27, 1976
HOMETOWN	TORRANCE, CALIFORNIA
ACTIVE YEARS	1997–2013

CAREER STATS

G: 270

REC: 1,325

REC YDS: 15,127

YDS/REC: 11.4

YDS/G: 56

REC TD: 111

PLAYOFF TD: 4

FUMBLES: 6

1ST DN: 866

CATCH %: 65.9

6X FIRST-TEAM ALL-PRO

2000s ALL-DECADE TEAM

14X PRO BOWL

"You have to play this game with a little bit of oomph. I call it courage. I call it confidence."

GLORY OR DEFEAT

On January 13, 2013, Tony Gonzalez reached the high point of his NFL career. He and the Atlanta Falcons had just defeated the Seattle Seahawks 30–28 to move on to the NFC Championship Game. After sixteen seasons in the NFL, Gonzalez finally got his first playoff win and was on the path to a Super Bowl.

He had only been to the playoffs five times in those fifteen seasons before but had never won. Gonzalez was already recognized as one of the greatest tight ends to play in the NFL, but he was missing one final piece: a Super Bowl win, a chance to stand on top of the mountain.

Sadly, life doesn't always have a fairy-tale ending. The Falcons lost the next week, and Gonzalez would never play another playoff game. He is one of the greatest players never to play in an NFL championship game. It may not seem fair, but in the end, none of that can take away from what Gonzalez achieved while he played. There is a lesson in that. Just playing the game can be the real reward and playing to your best ability is all that you can do.

TAKING A STAND

Gonzalez was born in California in 1976. He didn't grow up dreaming of being an NFL star. He just wanted to have fun and be a kid. It was his brother, Chris, who pushed Tony toward athletics. His brother was obsessed with football, so he brought Tony along.

A big moment for Gonzalez happened in eighth grade. Another kid had been bullying him, and he finally stood up to the bully. That gave him the confidence that would one day lead him to the NFL.

FROM BASKETBALL TO FOOTBALL

Once Gonzalez reached high school, he was a star athlete in both football and basketball. He thought that basketball would be his chosen sport when he was young. He was MVP of his league and even played in college. But he also played tight end and linebacker on the high school football team and was picked as an All-American player.

By 1994, it was time for college. Gonzalez went to the University of California, Berkeley. Like so many athletes before him, he was a two-sport star, but this time, football won out. His size, agility, and skill at catching the ball were rare for a tight end. He was so good that after his junior year, he decided to enter the NFL draft.

HIS TIME TO SHINE

During the 1997 draft, he went to the Kansas City Chiefs in the first round. He wasn't a star right from the start, but he was playing. Even when you're a star player in college, the NFL is different. It takes some time to learn the ropes. But by his third year in the NFL, Gonzalez really started to shine. He caught eleven touchdowns that year and began a long run of dominance.

Gonzalez was perfect for the tight end position. He was big enough that he could help block, but also fast enough to go out for passes. He always managed to locate the open spot for his quarterback to find him with the ball. His balance and speed allowed him to run that ball once he caught it. He even used his basketball skills on the field, with his height making it easy to catch the ball up high.

Gonzalez also owns a unique stat. He only fumbled six times in his whole career, and his team only lost two of those fumbles to the other team. But that's not the most amazing part of it. Five of his fumbles came in a two-year span (1998–1999), and for the other fifteen years of his career, he only fumbled once!

A TEAM PLAYER

Gonzalez set some impressive records. He had the most catches (1,325) and yards (15,127) by a tight end when he retired. To this day, only two players have more catches than Gonzalez: Jerry Rice (1,549) and Larry Fitzgerald (1,432). In 2004, Gonzalez led the league in catches, with 102. In all those years, he only missed two games.

Gonzalez retired after the 2013 season and was chosen for the Pro Football Hall of Fame in 2019. Since he stopped playing, he's been a sports announcer, actor, and author.

He never won that championship he was after, but Gonzalez was always there for his team and was always ready to give his best, win or lose. You can't always control the outcome of a game or a career, but you can control how much effort you put into it. No one ever doubted the effort Gonzalez put into the game.

FAST FACTS

- When he was a senior in high school, Tony Gonzalez shared the Orange County High School Athlete of the Year award with golfer Tiger Woods.

- Tony Gonzalez follows a plant-based diet and is mostly vegan. He wrote a book about his diet plan called *The All-Pro Diet: Lose Fat, Build Muscle, and Live Like a Champion.*

- Tony Gonzalez caught a pass in each of 211 straight games, starting on December 4, 2000, and ending on December 29, 2013, the final game of his career.

Runners-up

ROB GRONKOWSKI

Rob Gronkowski has spent his career winning Super
Bowls with Tom Brady, first with the New England
Patriots and then with the Tampa Bay Buccaneers. He's
won four Super Bowls and could still get another, as he
has not yet retired. He is one of the bigger tight ends
to ever play, but he is also one of the quickest, and he
became the first tight end ever to lead the league in
touchdowns, with seventeen in 2011.

ANTONIO GATES

Antonio Gates is an undrafted NFL player who overcame
the odds to become great. Undrafted players sign with
a team after the draft and have to work their way up the
roster to stay around. He played sixteen years for the San
Diego/Los Angeles Chargers (2003–2018). He was a basketball player coming out of college, but he picked up the
pro game quickly and skyrocketed from there. He went
on to play in eight Pro Bowls and was on the All-Decade
Team for the 2000s.

KELLEN WINSLOW

It is a shame that Kellen Winslow's career was cut short
by injury. He had the skills to be the best ever if he had
only had more time. But before a knee injury took him out
of the game, he played for the San Diego Chargers from

1979 to 1987 and was the main threat in an offense called Air Coryell under coach Don Coryell. He led the NFL in catches in 1980 and 1981.

Legendary Great

MIKE DITKA

Many sports fans today know Mike Ditka as the former coach of the Chicago Bears and New Orleans Saints and from his career as a sports announcer. But long before that, he was a football player for the University of Pittsburgh. Like so many other players, he was a star in different sports, but he was best at football by far, and in 1961, the Chicago Bears picked him in the draft.

He became a passing threat in a time when tight ends mostly blocked. His first year, he was named Rookie of the Year, and in 1963 he won the NFL title with the Bears. He also caught a touchdown while playing for the Dallas Cowboys in Super Bowl VI, which the Cowboys won.

Ditka picked up the nickname "Iron Mike" because he was from a steel town in Pennsylvania. But he was also a tough player who wasn't afraid of contact, so the nickname fit his style. Ditka was a fierce blocker, along with being a good receiver. He went on to win a Super Bowl as an assistant coach for the Cowboys and then as a head coach for the team he played on for six years, the Bears.

Mike Ditka

SHANNON SHARPE

Tight end Shannon Sharpe was one of the best ever to play that position, and he was also one of the biggest personalities the NFL has ever seen. Sharpe played for two teams in his fourteen years in the NFL: the Denver Broncos and the Baltimore Ravens.

Sharpe won three Super Bowls during his career, two with the Broncos (Super Bowls XXXII and XXXIII) and one with the Ravens (Super Bowl XXXV). He held the record for catches (815), yards (10,060), and touchdowns (62) by a tight end when he retired, but those records have since been broken.

Sharpe was one of the first of a new style of tight end. He only weighed around 228 pounds when he came into the league, which was small for a tight end. He had a body that wasn't typical for a receiver or a tight end. He didn't get picked until the seventh round of the draft in 1990. However, once the Broncos decided to make him a tight end, his career took off and he set the trend for future tight ends of his size.

ANTHONY MUÑOZ

OFFENSIVE TACKLE

JERSEY NUMBER	78
HEIGHT | WEIGHT	6' 6" | 278 LBS
BORN	AUGUST 19, 1958
HOMETOWN	ONTARIO, CALIFORNIA
ACTIVE YEARS	1980–1992

CAREER STATS*

G: 185   REC TD: 4

PLAYOFF G: 8

*Because offensive linemen rarely touch the ball and do not make tackles, there are very few stats for them. Instead of stats, we'll have to look at the traits that made them great.

NFL MAN OF THE YEAR (1991)

9X FIRST-TEAM ALL-PRO

11X PRO BOWL

"Anytime someone doubts you or suggests that maybe you should try another endeavor, there's the desire to show them you can do it."

A CHALLENGING START

When Anthony Muñoz was playing college football at the University of Southern California, he was having a big problem. Everyone knew that he was one of the best players at the school and that his talent had him heading for a big future. He was the perfect offensive lineman. Except for one thing: He could not stay healthy.

Muñoz suffered knee injuries in three of his four seasons at USC. In his senior year, he hurt his knee in the first game and everybody thought he was out for the season. When USC made the Rose Bowl, a game Muñoz had dreamed of playing in, no one believed it when he said he would be able to play in the game. But he did play, and he played very well. He made the big block on the touchdown that sent USC to the victory.

Some teams in the NFL doubted him because he was so injury prone. But the Cincinnati Bengals didn't, and they drafted him in 1980. Muñoz rewarded the Bengals with a Hall of Fame career, and he went on to be called the best offensive lineman ever.

He may have had obstacles early, but his belief in himself pulled him through. He never gave in to the injuries, or the doubters; he just worked his way back to playing.

PLAYING HARD

Muñoz was born in California in 1958. He was brought up in a home that didn't have a lot of money, but his mother made sure he had time to pursue sports instead of working on weekends to help the family. Even though Muñoz was big as a kid, he liked baseball over football.

When he did play flag football as a kid, he wasn't an offensive lineman. He was the quarterback. He was also a pitcher in baseball and said he liked throwing the ball in both sports.

NO LONGER A QUARTERBACK

Once he got to high school, he thought he would try out to be the quarterback, but the coach quickly changed him to an offensive lineman. That was a smart choice. In high school, Muñoz played baseball, basketball, and football. As he kept playing all three, it became clear that he had something special when it came to football.

He stayed close to home and chose the University of Southern California for college. He played both football and baseball there. While playing in college, he showed impressive skills that led him to the NFL. He won awards for All-American and All-Conference and was a member of the 1978 national championship team. But injuries were an issue coming out of college.

RISING ABOVE

As often as Muñoz was hurt in college, you might have expected the same to happen once he got to the NFL.

Instead, in his first twelve seasons, he missed only three games. The change in fortune from college to the pros was amazing.

Muñoz had every skill you would want in an offensive tackle. He was big, he was strong, he was smart, he was a hard worker, and he could really move his feet. Playing offensive tackle is about many things, but being able to quickly move your feet and keep your balance is a top priority. Muñoz was able to do that as well as any other tackle.

In his rookie season, he made the All-Rookie team. The next year, one opposing coach said that he couldn't believe it was only Muñoz's second year. He was that good! Most offensive lineman are either better at pass blocking or at run blocking. They usually have a strength. Muñoz did both at the highest level. He also caught seven passes in his career and scored four touchdowns.

In just about every season he played, he was voted Offensive Lineman of the Year. He went to two Super Bowls. Unfortunately, his luck ran out there and his team lost both. But he did join the Pro Football Hall of Fame in 1998.

EARNING RESPECT

When Muñoz retired, he created a charity that helps young people "mentally, physically, and spiritually." In

1991, he won the NFL Man of the Year award, which goes to the best both on and off the field. He is one of the most respected players ever.

He had overcome those days at USC when people wondered if he could keep playing football. But those early injuries also made him work harder. "In some ways, I think the injuries were a blessing," he said. "I had always taken my natural strength for granted. I had never worked at improving it. I now feel I'm quicker and stronger than ever."

That is how you make yourself one of the greatest NFL players ever, and one of the best people. When it came time for the Hall of Fame to name a former player to one of their board seats a few years back, the choice was easy. Here is what Hall of Fame president David Baker said: "A guy like Anthony, when he walks into a room, he commands the room. And it's because of his character and credibility. The logical guy was Anthony because he is respected so much by all the members. He's involved in so many charitable activities that build the character of kids."

Muñoz was a combination of everything you want in a football player. He was a terrific teammate and role model for the younger players. He had all the physical skills but kept working to make himself stronger. Off the field, he couldn't have been more admired. And when injuries threatened to derail his career, he fought back and became one of the best ever.

FAST FACTS

- Anthony Muñoz played college baseball and pitched for the University of Southern California's national championship team in 1978.

- It was said that Anthony Muñoz was so big as a kid they wouldn't let him play Pop Warner football because it was unfair to the other kids.

- When the Bengals coach came to scout Anthony Muñoz before the draft, they did some drills on the field, and Muñoz was so powerful that he accidentally knocked the coach to the ground.

Runners-up

BRUCE MATTHEWS

Bruce Matthews was an offensive lineman from 1983 to 2001 for the Houston Oilers/Tennessee Titans. He was so good that he played all five positions on the offensive line at different times and excelled at all of them. He was also the long snapper for kicks and punts. Matthews was picked for the Pro Bowl fourteen times, and he never missed a game for injury in 293 starts.

JONATHAN OGDEN

From 1996 through 2007, Jonathan Ogden was a top offensive tackle for the Baltimore Ravens. He went to the Pro Bowl every year except his first in the NFL. He was known for his big smile and easygoing way, but on the field, he wasn't afraid of contact with the defense. He also managed to catch two touchdowns and make ten tackles. He helped his team win Super Bowl XXXV.

LARRY ALLEN

It's quite possible that Larry Allen was the strongest man to ever play in the NFL. But he was also fast for an offensive lineman. He played with the Dallas Cowboys (1994–2005) and the San Francisco 49ers (2006–2007). As an offensive guard, he could push players around, but he could also pull outside to block. He won Super Bowl XXX with Dallas, and he was named to eleven Pro Bowls.

Legendary Great

JIM OTTO

No one really noticed Jim Otto's entry into pro football. No NFL team even drafted him, so he ended up in the rival American Football League (AFL) and signed with the Oakland Raiders.

For fifteen years, Otto was the man in the middle of the Raiders offensive line. He was an All-Star in the AFL every year. When that league joined the NFL, the awards kept coming. He was able to play for 210 games without missing one for injury. His team won the AFL championship in the 1967 season, but they ended up losing the Super Bowl to the Green Bay Packers.

His coach, another Hall of Famer named John Madden, said this about Otto: "His skills as a center were just perfect. He was one of those guys who never wanted to come out of practice. That's the opposite of most starters, who will say, 'Send in the second guy.' Jim was the Oakland Raiders center, and he wasn't going to give up his spot."

Otto may have flown under the radar at first. However, by the time his career was over, everybody had noticed him.

Spotlight

THE IMPORTANT JOB OF A CENTER

The center is sometimes called "the quarterback of the offensive line." They say that because, like the quarterback, the center has to read the defense and call out blocking directions for the rest of the offensive line. Reading a defense means seeing where the other team's defense is lined up and then deciding how to block its players based on that information. You have to be smart and think quickly to play center in the NFL.

Most fans know that the center's first job is to hike the ball between his legs to the quarterback. He has to do that every time and do it right, or the team could fumble the ball. He also has to block like the rest of the linemen. But before he does all that, he has to be able to read that defense, even when players are moving around and trying to trick him.

Not everyone can be a center. Some guys have the skills but don't have the mind to do what a center does. Others just never get a handle on snapping the ball correctly. Playing football is not easy, but when it comes to being a center, you may not find a more difficult position.

REGGIE WHITE

DEFENSIVE END

JERSEY NUMBER	92, 91
HEIGHT | WEIGHT	6' 5" | 300 LBS
BORN	DECEMBER 19, 1961
HOMETOWN	CHATTANOOGA, TENNESSEE
ACTIVE YEARS	1985–1998, 2000

CAREER STATS

G: 232

SACHS: 198

TACHLES: 1,111

INT: 3

FF: 33

FR: 20

TD: 2

PLAYOFF G: 19

PLAYOFF SACHS: 12

SAFETY: 1

2X DEFENSIVE PLAYER OF THE YEAR

8X FIRST-TEAM ALL-PRO

13X PRO BOWL

"There are no individuals on this team, and it feels good to be on a team that works toward the same goals, with guys that are unselfish."

A FREE AGENT

In today's NFL, players change teams all the time. Free agency comes every March, and players with contracts that have ended move around to new places. Earlier, we noted how Tom Brady had moved to the Tampa Bay Buccaneers after a long career with the Patriots. But did you know there was once a time when players couldn't do this?

All that changed in 1993, after Reggie White's court case started modern free agency. Players had been fighting for more freedom in choosing where they would play, and for how much, for a long time in the NFL, but the owners had all the power. They could keep players they wanted and negotiate contracts with them exclusively. When White won his court case in 1992, it forced the NFL to discuss a free agency plan for players. The agreed-upon plan led to players being able to negotiate with any team once their contracts ended, and it came into effect in 1993. That was the same year White left the Philadelphia Eagles for the Green Bay Packers. The rest, as they say, is history.

White's move to Green Bay stunned the NFL world. Green Bay had not had much success since the 1960s under head coach Vince Lombardi. Not only was Wisconsin freezing cold, it was also a small TV market. Not many players were lining up to play in Green Bay, but White did. And by doing that, he changed the fortunes of the Packers, who before long went from losers to big winners. Then every player wanted to be in Green Bay, and they became big winners. No wonder every Packers fan loves White!

This is what Packers assistant coach Greg Blache had to say about that time: "Everybody suspected [Reggie White would] go to a big city for outside endorsements. But [Assistant Coach] Ray Rhodes did a phenomenal job of recruiting Reggie. I think it blew everybody's mind that he would come to Green Bay. It set the tone. He was the premier guy, and it turned the tables to where guys didn't just run to the big market."

A HIGHER CALLING

White changed the NFL—and not just with his play. He was also someone who knew exactly what he wanted to do in life. His mother says that at twelve years of age, White stated he wanted to be two things in life: a football player and a minister. He would go on to do both.

"When I was a child, I was always bigger than the other kids," White told *Sports Illustrated*. "Kids used to call me Bigfoot or Land of the Giant. They'd tease me and run away. Around seventh grade, I found something I was good at. I could play football, and I could use my size and achieve success by playing within the rules. I remember telling my mother that someday I would be a professional football player and I'd take care of her for the rest of her life."

THE MINISTER OF DEFENSE

Deeply religious, Reggie White became a minister at the age of seventeen. Soon after that, he was playing college football at Tennessee. These two passions came together to give him his nickname, "The Minister of Defense."

During White's years at Tennessee, he was a star. He was a cut above most players, and everyone was sure he would end up in the NFL. During his senior year, he intercepted a pass, got one hundred tackles, and made fifteen sacks.

AN IMPORTANT CHOICE

At the time, there were other football leagues outside the NFL. One was called the U.S. Football League (USFL). In 1984, the Memphis Showboats, a team in that league, drafted White. But the NFL was too powerful, and the USFL eventually folded a few years later. But the NFL was paying attention, and White joined the Philadelphia Eagles.

For eight seasons White was a star in Philadelphia, but in 1993, his contract ended. Because of the court case he had won, he could now pick a new team. White became the first big-name free agent to change teams, and he went on to help the Packers win Super Bowl XXXI. He made the right choice!

CHANGING THE GAME

In all, White played for the Eagles, Packers, and one year with the Carolina Panthers. He won one Super Bowl and was named the Defensive Player of the Year twice (1987 and 1998). He finished his career with 198 sacks, the record until Bruce Smith broke it with 200. It took Smith forty-seven more games than White to get to that number. From 1985 to 1993, White had ten or more sacks each year, a record of nine seasons that still stands.

White died on December 26, 2004 and was voted into the Hall of Fame in 2006. He had changed the game, first by his amazing playing, then in how players got to choose where they played. Free agency turned out to be a game changer for the sport. It was good for the players, the fans, the teams, and even the league. What was already an exciting sport became something even White couldn't have anticipated. Can you imagine how different the league would have been without him?

FAST FACTS

- In 2005, the Philadelphia Eagles, the Green Bay Packers, and the University of Tennessee all retired Reggie White's jersey number.

- When Reggie White was deciding which team to play for in 1993, he said he would go with God in his decision. It has been said that Packers Coach Mike Holmgren then called White, got his answering machine, and left this message: "Reggie, this is God. Come to Green Bay."

- At Tennessee in 1981, Reggie White blocked three extra points in one season.

Runners-up

BRUCE SMITH

Bruce Smith was the Defensive Player of the Year in 1990 and 1996. He holds the NFL record for 200 sacks. He was the first overall pick of the Buffalo Bills in 1985 and was a nine-time All-Pro. He went to four Super Bowls, but his team lost them all.

AARON DONALD

Aaron Donald is still an active player with the Los Angeles Rams and won Super Bowl LVI. He is already considered among the best defensive tackles to ever play, and he's not done yet. His strength and quickness make him very hard to block, so every game, the other team ends up focusing a lot of attention on him.

JOE GREENE

"Mean" Joe Greene is one of the greatest nicknames, but he was actually a very nice guy. He was also a terrific defensive tackle who played for the Pittsburgh Steelers in the 1970s and won four Super Bowls. Everyone knew his Coke commercial, in which he threw his jersey to a fan who offered him a Coke after a tough game. Doesn't sound mean at all!

Legendary Great

DEACON JONES

If you want to know how the NFL came up with the term "sack" for tackling the quarterback, you have to go to Deacon Jones. There have been different stories about how he came up with the name. The best one is that before his team played against quarterback Craig Morton (like the famous salt brand), he said they were going to "pour that Morton salt into a sack." The term stuck and is credited to Jones.

Jones was chosen in the fourteenth round of the 1961 draft. He played for three different teams but was most famous for his time with the Los Angeles Rams (1961–1971). They called his defensive line the "Fearsome Foursome" because other teams feared going up against them.

Besides naming the sack, Jones was famous for another thing: the "head slap." He would hit the blocker in the helmet to gain an advantage. He was so good at it that they ended up making it illegal after he retired.

Deacon Jones

BEST DEFENSIVE LINE

1971 Vikings: Carl Eller, Alan Page, Jim Marshall, Gary Larsen

Many believe the best defensive line ever was the "Purple People Eaters." Doesn't sound like a football team, right? The term came from a pop song in the 1950s and was used because the Minnesota Vikings' team color is purple. Their motto was "meet at the quarterback." Would you want to be that quarterback?

The Purple People Eaters were the kind of players who liked to create big plays. They weren't happy just making tackles. They wanted to create turnovers, or get big sacks, or even block a field goal. They were known for their quickness and agility instead of their size. No matter which offensive player had the ball, one of them was likely closing in for the hit.

Their greatest season was 1971. Carl Eller was given the Defensive Player of the Year award. Topping that, Alan Page became the first ever defensive player to win the NFL MVP award. He is still the only defensive lineman to win that award. Both Page and Eller are in the Pro Football Hall of Fame.

DICK BUTKUS

LINEBACKER

JERSEY NUMBER	51
HEIGHT | WEIGHT	6' 3" | 245 LBS
BORN	DECEMBER 9, 1942
HOMETOWN	CHICAGO, ILLINOIS
ACTIVE YEARS	1965–1973

CAREER STATS

G: 119

G STARTED: 119

TACKLES (ESTIMATED): 1,020

INT: 22

FR: 25

TD: 1

SAFETY: 1

XP MADE: 2

SACKS and FORCED FUMBLES weren't official stats during the time Butkus played, but his numbers were high.

2X DEFENSIVE PLAYER OF THE YEAR (1969, 1970)

5X FIRST-TEAM ALL-PRO

8X PRO BOWL

" . . . society says you . . . had to be fierce. I was fierce. Tough. I was tough."

AN EXTRA POINT

Linebacker Dick Butkus was one of the most feared defenders to ever play football. He was mean, intimidating, and ready to crush running backs. You might think his favorite play was probably one where he caused a fumble, or tackled a runner, or sacked a quarterback—something physical and fast. Instead, his favorite play was on special teams, and it was one you never saw coming.

It happened on November 14, 1971, in a game against Washington. The Bears had just tied the game 15–15 in the fourth quarter. As they lined up for the extra point, a bad snap went rolling on the ground and was picked up by the Bears' holder, Bobby Douglass. Butkus was lined up on the end of the line as a blocker on the play. He saw what happened and took off for the end zone.

Somehow, Douglass eluded the Washington players long enough to heave a pass to the end zone. There, in the corner, a diving Butkus caught the ball as he hit the ground. The extra point was good, and the Bears hung on to win the game.

But that's how Butkus played the game, always going 100 percent and doing whatever he could to win, even if it wasn't his role. He typically played defense, where he had made that reputation as the meanest guy on the field. A rough linebacker rarely had the chance to score an extra point. But it wasn't the last time he did it. A year later, he made the exact same play. No wonder it was his favorite.

CHICAGO RAISED

Butkus was born in Chicago and hardly left the state of Illinois. Butkus knew he wanted to be a professional football player at an early age. Even though he would one day play for the Chicago Bears, as a kid he rooted for the other pro team in town during that time—the Chicago Cardinals.

AN ALL-STATE PLAYER

Butkus attended a high school that was quite a distance from his home because its football coach had gone to Notre Dame, a powerhouse school for football. He was an All-State player in high school and also played fullback on offense, in addition to defense.

Butkus stood out in college at Illinois. He was on the All-America team as a center in 1963 and finished third in the Heisman Trophy vote. He played both center on offense and linebacker on defense. He received numerous awards, not only for his play at linebacker, but also for his play at center. He also won the college football Player of the Year award in 1964.

A DREAM COME TRUE

Butkus was drafted by the Chicago Bears in 1965. Guess he liked it in Illinois! Everyone knew he was good in college, but they didn't know just how good until he arrived in the pros. The Bears already had a middle linebacker named Bill George when Butkus first arrived. George would go on to the Hall of Fame, so he was no slouch, but when Dick arrived, Bill said, "I started packing my gear. I knew my Bear days were numbered. There was no way that guy wasn't going to be great."

Butkus became the linebacker every future linebacker measured themselves against. For a long time, he was the agreed-upon best to ever play. He could run from sideline to sideline but was also a very big man and had a rough way of playing the game. Other players admitted they were a little scared of him. No wonder the nickname for the Bears defense at that time was "Monsters of the Midway."

Dave Osborn, a tough running back on an opposing team, said this about Butkus: "With my running style, when I got hit by a linebacker, I usually could drag him two yards. When Butkus hit me, I'd go backwards two yards."

Another running back, MacArthur Lane, said of Butkus: "If I had a choice, I'd sooner go one-on-one with a grizzly bear. I prayed that I could get up every time Butkus hit me." But Butkus wasn't all brawn. Middle linebackers were the quarterbacks of the defense in those days and were usually responsible for making the play calls on defense. They had to be smart about the game, even before a play began.

"I look first at the formation," Butkus said. "Then, I look to see if a halfback is cheating a few inches. I look at the halfback's eyes, and then the quarterback's eyes and head. Some jokers, they throw in the first direction they look. I may decide at the last second that I'm gonna call a stunt, or that I'm gonna shoot. If I shoot, the thing I hope is that I get a good angle on the runner, or if I've played the pass that I can strip the guy down and make him drop the ball. That takes it outta guys."

A CAREER CUT SHORT

Butkus only got to play nine seasons in the NFL because a severe knee injury eventually forced him to retire. Even so, in that time, he was twice the Defensive Player of the Year (1969 and 1970), he went to eight Pro Bowls, and he was named First-Team All-Pro five times.

His jarring hits forced numerous fumbles, and he recovered twenty-seven of them, a record when he retired. He finished his career with twenty-two interceptions. He was large but could still be quick and nimble when he needed to be. He could run with running backs and tight ends in coverage.

He combined every skill you needed for a middle linebacker into one package. The league hadn't seen anything like him before. He redefined what it meant to be a middle linebacker in the NFL. Linebackers are expected to be big, fast, and able to read a defense. They also need to cover receivers. He raised the standard for the position.

FAST FACTS

- In high school, Dick Butkus had an unusual way of training: by pushing a car up and down a street to strengthen his legs.

- Butkus made sure he was ready to play by making himself mad. "When I went out on the field to warm up, I would manufacture things to make me mad. If someone on the other team was laughing, I'd pretend he was laughing at me or the Bears. It always worked for me," he said.

- Once Dick Butkus retired, he went on to another career as an actor. He was in numerous films, including *Gremlins 2* and *Necessary Roughness*, and did a series of classic commercials with fellow football star Bubba Smith.

Runners-up

MIKE SINGLETARY

The Chicago Bears have had some of the very best linebackers in the NFL. Mike Singletary played for them from

1981 to 1992 and won a Super Bowl for the 1985 season. He was known for the intense look in his eyes just before a play was about to start. He was the Defensive Player of the Year in 1985 and 1988 and went to ten Pro Bowls. He also became an NFL head coach for the San Francisco 49ers.

JACK LAMBERT

Jack Lambert played his career for the Pittsburgh Steelers from 1974 to 1984. He won four Super Bowls and went to nine Pro Bowls. He was as good playing against the run as he was in covering passes. Lambert lost his four front teeth in a basketball game in high school. He wore dentures, but not during games, which gave him a unique look on the field.

DERRICK THOMAS

In eleven seasons with the Kansas City Chiefs (1989–1999), Derrick Thomas was one of the best pass rushers ever for an outside linebacker. He won the NFL Man of the Year award in 1993. He went to nine Pro Bowls and had 126.5 sacks before his death in a car accident while he was still with the Chiefs. There is no doubt that he would have set many more records had he lived.

Legendary Great

CHUCK BEDNARIK

Chuck Bednarik played linebacker for the Philadelphia Eagles from 1949 to 1962. He won two NFL titles and was a First-Team All-Pro nine times. Before he joined the NFL, he used to sell concrete for a living, hence his nickname, Concrete Charlie.

Bednarik is remembered for a special reason. He was one the last players who played both offense and defense. That was a common thing early on in the NFL, but by the end of Bednarik's career, almost all players were either offense or defense only.

He played center on offense and linebacker on defense. Even though he would play almost the entire game, he only missed three games in fourteen years. He was known for being a tough player who really liked to hit the offense when he was playing linebacker. But he also received All-NFL awards as a center.

Chuck Bednarik

When Bednarik retired, an era when players would play on both sides of the ball came to an end. Some have done a little of that, but Bednarik set the standard as a truly versatile player.

Special Mention

LAWRENCE TAYLOR

Lawrence Taylor is considered the greatest linebacker by many for what he did on the field. Off the field, Taylor had a lot of problems with the law. If not for that, he probably would have been considered the greatest here. But in comparison to the other players listed, there is less to celebrate.

During his playing days, he was almost impossible to block as an outside linebacker and was always in the backfield of the offense. He won two Super Bowls and was the NFL MVP in 1986. He played from 1981 to 1993 with the New York Giants.

DEION SANDERS

CORNERBACK

JERSEY NUMBER   **21**
HEIGHT | WEIGHT   **6' 1" | 200 LBS**
BORN   **AUGUST 9, 1967**
HOMETOWN   **FORT MYERS, FLORIDA**
ACTIVE YEARS   **1989–2000 AND 2004–2005**

CAREER STATS

G: **188**

INT: **53**

FF: **10**

TACHLES: **512**

PR YDS: **2,199**

PR TD: **6**

KR YDS: **3,523**

KR TD: **3**

REC: **60**

REC TD: **3**

1994 DEFENSIVE PLAYER OF THE YEAR

6X FIRST-TEAM ALL-PRO

8X PRO BOWL

"If you don't believe in yourself, how will somebody else believe in you?"

TWO IN ONE

On October 11, 1992, something happened that had never been done before. It may be something that will never be done again, and it certainly changed sports.

Deion Sanders put on a uniform for two different teams, in two different pro sports. On the same day. Can you imagine? That day, Sanders played a football game in Miami for the Atlanta Falcons. His team didn't win, but it was already a memorable day for Deion. He had played as a cornerback and played well. He also returned two kick-offs and one punt and caught a nine-yard pass on offense.

But his day wasn't over! He took a helicopter to the airport and flew to Pittsburgh, where he suited up for the Atlanta Braves in a playoff game against the Pirates. The Braves lost, and Sanders sat on the bench and never played. Still, he had done what no one had done before—two states, two teams, two sports, one day.

DOING IT ALL

Sanders doing it all started when he was young in Florida. As a child, Sanders liked to play both baseball and foot-ball. He grew up in a rough neighborhood, so his mother pushed him to play sports to keep him out of trouble.

His Pop Warner coach said when he first met nine-year-old Sanders, he weighed only 85 pounds but could run like a deer. That same coach also let him know that playing sports would keep him from the trouble some of his friends were getting into at the time. Sanders added basketball to the sports he played, and soon he was starting on multiple teams.

NEVER RESTING

Neon Deion and Prime Time—those were the nicknames Sanders had because of his amazing athletic skills. And that day in October noted earlier was not the only time Sanders had done something like that!

You name the sport, and he played it: football, basketball, baseball, and track. He was so good in baseball that the Kansas City Royals drafted him right out of high school, but he went to college at Florida State University instead. And he did it all there, too! He was named All-American in football and earned a Jim Thorpe Award. He also took home a conference championship in track and won a championship game in baseball.

In 1987, while Sanders was still in college, his baseball team and track team were playing in sporting events in the same city. Sanders played a baseball game, then moved on to run a track event, then went back and played in another baseball game. Maybe they could have added Do-It-All Deion to his list of nicknames.

FROM THE WORLD SERIES TO THE SUPER BOWL

When the Atlanta Falcons drafted him, Sanders also played for the New York Yankees. That season, he scored a touchdown and hit a home run in the same week!

Sanders went on to play baseball part-time for nine seasons while still playing football at the same time. Football was his main focus, and it was easy to see why. He became what many would describe as the finest cover corner to ever play. He used his unmatched skills to blanket receivers, and he was among the best to return punts and kickoffs on special teams.

If you look at the all-time interception leaders in the NFL, Sanders is low on the list. Interceptions are one way to measure a cornerback, but the reason his totals were low is because quarterbacks refused to throw the ball to who he was covering. He was too good, so he had fewer chances to get an interception.

Adding to his do-it-all list, Sanders was one of the best special-teams players in the game. During the 1992 season, he led the NFL in kick return yards (1,067) and average return yards for each kick (26.7). He even scored two touchdowns while on special teams that season.

In 1994, after he moved to the San Francisco 49ers, he won the Defensive Player of the Year award and got an interception in Super Bowl XXIX, which the 49ers won. He eventually played for the Dallas Cowboys and won the Super Bowl with them the next year. One reason he signed with Dallas was that they offered him the chance to play offense as a receiver. There's practically nothing he hasn't done!

In that Super Bowl win for the Cowboys, Sanders caught a forty-seven-yard pass. He was also the first to catch a pass and get an interception in the Super Bowl, and he was the first to play in both a Super Bowl and a World Series.

NO LIMITS

On top of all his accomplishments, Sanders had a huge personality. He was funny and charming, starring in many television commercials. He also put out a music album and appeared on TV as a broadcaster after he was done playing.

Sanders didn't believe in limiting what he could do. He played football for the Falcons, 49ers, Cowboys, Washington Redskins, and the Baltimore Ravens. In baseball, he played for the Yankees, Braves, Cincinnati Reds, and the San Francisco Giants. That's nine teams across two sports in fifteen years. He proved that such a thing wasn't just a dream, but a reality. He really did it all!

FAST FACTS

- Since 2020, Deion Sanders has been the head football coach at Jackson State in the Football Championship Subdivision level of college football. In 2021 the team went 11–2 and won the conference title.

- Deion Sanders never met a camera he didn't like and hosted an episode of *Saturday Night Live* on February 18, 1995.

- Deion Sanders is one of only two players to score touchdowns six different ways (rushing, receiving, interception return, punt return, kickoff return, and fumble recovery). Bill Dudley is the other.

Runners-up

ROD WOODSON

Rod Woodson played in the NFL for seventeen seasons (1987–2003) and won Super Bowl XXXV with the Baltimore Ravens. He is the NFL's leader on defense for fumble recoveries (32) and was the 1993 Defensive Player of the Year. He has seventy-one interceptions, which puts him in third place for all time.

MEL BLOUNT

From 1970 to 1983, Mel Blount was considered the best corner in the game. He won four Super Bowls in the 1970s with the Steelers. Blount was known for a physical style of covering players. The NFL even changed the rules so corners couldn't be so aggressive, or it would be pass interference. The so-called Mel Blount Rule didn't stop him, as he just adjusted his style.

CHARLES WOODSON

Charles Woodson (no relation to Rod) played for the Oakland Raiders and the Green Bay Packers. He was the Defensive Player of the Year in 2009. He also won Super Bowl XLV with Green Bay. He is tied with two other players for all-time touchdowns on defense (13) and is tied for fifth in most interceptions (65).

Legendary Great

DICK "NIGHT TRAIN" LANE

Great nickname alert! Dick "Night Train" Lane played in the NFL from 1952 through 1965 for the Los Angeles Rams, Chicago Cardinals, and Detroit Lions. The main thing you need to know about Lane is that he set a record with fourteen interceptions in his rookie year. At that time, the season was only twelve games and they threw the ball a lot less than they do today. Now it's seventeen games a season, but his record still stands!

Lane totaled sixty-eight interceptions in his career, which is still fourth all-time today. He's also noted for something cornerbacks don't usually do well. He was a very hard hitter when tackling. His tackles were so rough around the head and neck area that they changed the rules because they were afraid he was going to hurt other players.

He was a seven-time All-Pro, and he went to seven Pro Bowls in his career. He joined the Pro Football Hall of Fame in 1974 and was a member of the 1950s All-Decade Team.

Honorable Mention

CHAMP BAILEY

During his career, Champ Bailey played for Washington and Denver. He was a first-round draft pick and was widely considered the best corner of his generation. He was picked for twelve Pro Bowls, which is the most ever for a cornerback.

He had a standout year in 2006, when he grabbed ten interceptions and did not give up a touchdown pass. He finished second for Defensive Player of the Year. That year, he was involved in a very memorable play. During a playoff game, he intercepted a Tom Brady pass in the endzone and ran it all the way back to the one-yard line of the Patriots. Bailey is remembered as much for his brains as his physical skills. On the aforementioned play, it is said he changed the coverage because he recognized what the play was going to be, and that allowed him to intercept the ball. He was also noted as a very good tackler. He entered the Pro Football Hall of Fame in 2019.

Champ Bailey

RONNIE LOTT

SAFETY

JERSEY NUMBER **42**
HEIGHT | WEIGHT **6' 0" | 203 LBS**
BORN **MAY 8, 1959**
HOMETOWN **ALBUQUERQUE, NEW MEXICO**
ACTIVE YEARS **1981–1994**

CAREER STATS

G: 192

INT: 63

FR: 17

FF: 16

TACKLES: 1,146

TD: 5

PLAYOFF G: 20

PLAYOFF INT: 9

PLAYOFF TD: 2

SACKS: 8.5

4X SUPER BOWL WINNER
8X FIRST-TEAM ALL-PRO
10X PRO BOWL

*"It's easy to help others, to give them hope,
some belief that they can make it.
You've got to share yourself."*

SACRIFICE AND BALANCE

In sports discussions, there is always talk about the players giving it all for the game—leaving 100 percent on the field after doing everything possible to prepare. That might have been what was crossing Ronnie Lott's mind when he gave doctors permission to remove the tip of his pinky.

Lott had shattered the tip of the bone in his pinky in the last game of the 1985 season. Doctors said they could put a pin in it, put it in a cast, and wait for it to heal. There was just one problem. Lott's team, the San Francisco 49ers, were playing in the playoffs the next week, and Lott wanted to play. The doctors said he would be able play but could lose his pinky. It was an extreme choice and the doctors didn't recommend it, but Lott chose to play.

After all that, the 49ers lost that playoff game, and doctors had to remove the top part of his pinky so he could play in 1986 without missing time. Soon, Lott came to regret his decision. He realized that athletes need to be smart about their bodies. He still believed in giving it your all, working hard, and being there for the team. But he realized you have to be mindful about your choices and think long term. That is a lesson we could all learn—that there is always balance in life.

A MILITARY KID

Lott was part of a military family that moved around a lot when he was young. As a child, he loved all kinds of sports and used to watch any sport he could find on television. He also played on Pee Wee football teams and on his junior high school's teams. It was in junior high that he started to work on his aggressive tackling, something he became known for in the NFL.

A WINNING RECORD

Lott ended up in high school in California and was a star in football, basketball, and baseball. He played those sports for three years. He was named an All-American in football by *Parade* magazine. He played against Anthony Muñoz in high school, and they would go on to be teammates in college.

He thought he wanted to go to the University of California, Los Angeles, because of their powerhouse basketball program, but he chose football and the University of Southern California instead. At USC, he was a star and received an All-American honor. In the 1978 season, Lott and USC only lost one game and were awarded the national championship. The next season, they didn't lose any games and tied one.

WHATEVER IT TAKES

The San Francisco 49ers drafted Lott and he was a starter right away, leading the team to a win in Super Bowl XVI. In that rookie season, he was still playing as a cornerback, and he returned three interceptions for touchdowns.

A few years later, the 49ers moved Lott to the position of safety, which turned out to be a smart move. Lott's career really took off, and he became one of the greatest safeties ever. He was a versatile player, and whatever the team needed to win, Lott would do. Free safety was what he did best, but he could also play left and right corner-back and strong safety. Eventually, he went to the Pro Bowl playing all those positions.

He was known for his rugged, physical style of play. He was a hard hitter, but he was also a smart player. He just knew which way a play was going. That was mostly because he studied offenses so he could get clues about what they were going to do. Once he had it figured out, he used everything he had to stop the play.

"You get the hits because you learn the angles and you learn the angles because you're so immersed in the game, so in love with it, you're always learning. You end up understanding things other players don't understand, seeing things other players don't see," he said.

In one of his best seasons, he had ten interceptions and led the league. He also caused three fumbles while getting his seventy-seven tackles. By the time Lott finished in San Francisco, the team had won four Super Bowls. At the end of his career, he played a few seasons with the Oakland Raiders, and even then, he led the league in interceptions. Then he played two seasons with the New York Jets before retiring.

Famous Dallas Cowboys head coach Tom Landry said of Lott: "He's devastating. He may dominate the secondary better than anyone I've seen."

FINISHING STRONG

Eight-time All-Pro, ten Pro Bowls, sixty-three interceptions, five returns for touchdowns, four Super Bowls, and the respect of his peers—those are tough stats to beat.

Getting rid of his pinky all those years ago wasn't the best idea. But everything else he did was the best. He could tackle, he could get interceptions, and he could think his way through a play. He was at the very top of the game and left a career that is among the best we have seen, even without his pinky.

FAST FACTS

- The reason Ronnie Lott wore jersey number 42 was because his favorite player growing up was Washington receiver Charley Taylor. Lott took his number for his jersey.

- When Ronnie Lott was eleven years old, his Pee Wee team, the San Bernardino Jets, outscored their opponents by a margin of 377–22 in winning all ten of their games.

- When Ronnie Lott was at the University of Southern California, he had some famous teammates. Anthony Muñoz (Hall of Fame), Marcus Allen (Hall of Fame), Bruce Matthews (Hall of Fame), Dennis Smith (NFL great), and Jeff Fisher (NFL player/head coach) were just some of the future NFL players on that roster.

Runners-up

ED REED

Ed Reed played most of his career for the Baltimore Ravens (2002-2012) and was the 2004 Defensive Player of the Year. He holds the record for most return yards off interceptions (1,590) and had returns of 106 and 107 yards! He is the model of a "ball-hawk" safety, a player who attacks the football.

KEN HOUSTON

Ken Houston played safety for (what a coincidence!) Houston (1967–1972) and Washington (1973–1980). He went to twelve Pro Bowls and was voted onto the 1970s All-Decade Team. He always had a sense of where the football was going. He was noted for what he could do with the ball in his hands after interceptions or fumbles, turning defense into offense.

PAUL KRAUSE

Paul Krause's last season was in 1979, but he still holds the NFL record for interceptions with eighty-one. He played with both Washington and Minnesota and led the league in interceptions (12) in his rookie year. He played in four Super Bowls, but the Vikings never won.

Legendary Great

EMLEN TUNNELL

Many younger football fans have never heard of Emlen Tunnell. He played from 1948 to 1961, a long time ago. But every NFL fan should know his name. He was the first Black player to be voted into the Pro Football Hall of Fame and to play for the New York Giants.

Tunnell played for the Giants until 1958 and then with the Green Bay Packers until he retired in 1961. He left the league with the record for interceptions, at seventy-nine. He was also a great special-teams player and held the record for punt return yards (2,209). Those records have been broken, but at the time, they were unbelievable!

Off the field, his feats were just as impressive. Before joining the NFL, Tunnell served in the Coast Guard and was noted for saving the lives of two people. In 2021, the Coast Guard named one of their ships after him.

He won championships in 1956 and 1961, then became an assistant coach and joined the Pro Football Hall of Fame in 1967. Even though it was a long time ago, he is still one of the greats.

Emlen Tunnell

STRONG SAFETY VS. FREE SAFETY

The safety position is usually at the very back of the defense. They are called the last line of defense. Sometimes, there are two safeties back there, a free safety and a strong safety. Other times, there is only one that far back, the free safety, while the strong safety is playing closer to the line of scrimmage.

Most of the time, the free safety is the lighter, quicker one of the two. He plays at the very back and tries to keep any receiver from getting past him. He needs to be fast enough to run with the receivers and cover them. He also needs to be ready to make a tackle if the runner gets past the front of the defense.

The strong safety is usually a little bigger. He sometimes stays back to cover receivers, but he can also move closer to the line of scrimmage. He might be used to help stop running plays, or he could cover running backs and tight ends like an extra linebacker. He can also be used to blitz the quarterback.

In the modern NFL, safeties have become more similar and sometimes play at both positions. In the past, they were more defined in the two positions, but it's common to see players switching between the two spots today.

JUSTIN TUCKER

KICKER

JERSEY NUMBER 9
HEIGHT | WEIGHT 6' 1" | 183 LBS
BORN NOVEMBER 21, 1989
HOMETOWN HOUSTON, TEXAS
ACTIVE YEARS 2012–PRESENT

CAREER STATS

(Through the 2021–2022 season)

G: 161

FG ATT: 358

FG MADE: 326

FG%: 91.1

XP ATT: 386

XP MADE: 382

XP%: 99

KO: 885

TB%: 61.9

50+ FG MADE: 48

NFL ALL-2010s TEAM

5X FIRST-TEAM ALL-PRO

5X PRO BOWL

"It's about thinking about the action and not the consequence."

PERFORMING UNDER PRESSURE

Kickers don't get a lot of field time, so when they do, there's often a lot riding on that moment. But that's what kickers live for. Kick a field goal and win the game at the last second? You got it. Do it from, say, fifty yards away? No problem. Now do it while attempting a record sixty-six-yard kick? That may be asking too much. But not for one kicker in particular.

At a game in late September 2021, the Baltimore Ravens needed their kicker to do the impossible: kick sixty-six yards in the dying seconds of a game against the Detroit Lions. You have to give head coach John Harbaugh credit for even having the guts to call the play. But he had a good reason to do it: Justin Tucker.

Tucker went through his routine before taking the field, but in this situation, he thought his normal routine might not be the best approach. "When you're that far away . . . you have to abandon a certain amount of your technique . . . to gain a little power and use the adrenaline and the feeling of the moment to get the ball to go. I hop into it just a little more aggressively," he said.

He knew he would need a little extra something. And it was a good thing he changed it up. His kick had just enough distance to hit the crossbar and bounce through. The Ravens won 19–17, and the NFL had a new record for the longest field goal ever.

KICKING IT OFF

Kicking field goals and scoring points is nothing new for Tucker. When he was eleven years old, he would kick a ball through the limbs of an oak tree in his backyard. The trunk of the tree split into a Y shape, and Tucker used it as his first goal posts. He started playing football in junior high school after switching from soccer. At first, he was used in other positions, but when the coach went looking for a kicker, Tucker volunteered.

Once his family realized how good he was at it, they brought in a kicking coach to work with him when he was fifteen. That is when he really started to take off as a kicker. His skills improved from the coaching and his own desire to practice all the time.

DOWN TO THE WIRE

In high school, Justin was the team's kicker as well as a receiver and a safety. Of course, with that leg, he also played soccer.

Once he got to college at the University of Texas, he became their punter and kicker. Proving he knew about game-winning kicks early on, he knocked in a forty-yard kick in the last second to defeat rival Texas A&M University. But like most kickers, even with all his success at Texas, he went undrafted.

AN UNBEATABLE ROUTINE

Eventually, Tucker signed with the Ravens in 2012, and has played with them ever since, probably because he proved to be such an asset right from the start. In his third game in the NFL, he kicked a field goal to win the game. He hasn't stopped doing that since.

Players face a lot of pressure as the clock is winding down, but Tucker handles it through rigorous practice. He has his kicking routine down. He knows exactly what to do each time he is out there because he has prepared for every possibility, and he stays focused on the present moment.

"Whenever we're fortunate enough to have a game-winning field goal opportunity, especially a walk-off, I get more nervous *after* the fact thinking about what if that didn't go the way we wanted it to go," he said.

You can only control what you are doing in the moment. Thinking about the win or loss isn't going to help. But preparation makes those moments a lot less nerve wracking. That has certainly worked for Tucker. He is the most accurate kicker in the history of the game, ever. He makes just over 91 percent of his field goals and around 99 percent of his extra points—short kicks, long kicks, and everything in between, too. He's made more than 72 percent of his field goals from more than fifty yards, whereas the league average is closer to 65 percent.

THE CLOSER

In the playoffs leading up to Super Bowl XLVII, he made a forty-seven-yard field goal in overtime to win the game. Then, when the Ravens were playing in the big game, Tucker made two field goals in the fourth quarter and helped take the team to victory.

When the pressure is on, Justin Tucker doesn't crack. He relies on his practice, his routine, and his technique. He stays in the moment instead of thinking of what can happen afterward. He keeps his focus and just does what he knows he should be doing—kicking field goals. He's so good at it that his teammate, Mark Andrews, simply says this about Tucker: "That's the GOAT."

FAST FACTS

- Tucker majored in music in college and said that if he wasn't in the NFL, he'd like to be the lead singer of an '80s hair rock cover band.

- He can sing opera as a baritone in several different languages. Check him out online singing "Ave Maria."

- As part of his pre-game routine, Tucker lays out his whole uniform on the locker room floor in the shape of a person.

RAY GUY

Ray Guy is the greatest punter the NFL has ever seen. In 1973, he became the first punter who didn't play any other position to be taken in the first round of the draft. He played his career with the Oakland/Los Angeles Raiders (1973–1986) and was known for punts that went so high that by the time they were caught, his team was already in position to make the tackle.

MORTEN ANDERSEN

Born in Denmark, Morten Andersen was given the nickname "Great Dane." He kicked in the NFL for twenty-five seasons (1982–2007) and played in more games (382) than any player ever. He played his final game when he was forty-seven years old. Andersen is second in all-time points scored, with 2,544.

ADAM VINATIERI

Adam Vinatieri was known as one of the most skilled clutch kickers of all time. When it counted at the end of the game, Adam Vinatieri almost never missed. He won four Super Bowls—three with the New England Patriots and one with the Indianapolis Colts. He is the NFL's all-time leading scorer, with 2,673 points.

Beating the Odds

FEMALE KICKERS

Football teams have historically been all male, but a few pioneering women have made it into the game at the college level.

Liz Heaston became the first woman to ever score in a college football game. She kicked two extra points for Willamette University on October 18, 1997. She was a soccer player at the school when she tried out as a kicker and ended up appearing in two games.

Becca Longo achieved another first for women in football. She was the kicker on her high school team, and her skills earned her a free ride to Adams State University.

Sarah Fuller

Injuries cut her career short, but she helped pave the way for women in football.

Sarah Fuller is known as the first woman to play in a college game between two Power 5 schools. On November 28, 2020, Fuller kicked off for the Vanderbilt Commodores against the Missouri Tigers. Two weeks later, she became the first woman to score in a game between two Power 5 teams when she kicked an extra point against Tennessee.

Given how women have progressed in college football, the next step will be for a tryout in the NFL. As women come up through soccer programs, they can try out as kickers, and one day, a woman will take her shot at the NFL.

Spotlight

NFL CAREER POINTS LEADERS

When fans think about their football teams, they rarely think about the kickers. They should. If you look at the list of all-time leading scorers in the NFL, the first non-kicker you will see is Jerry Rice, at number 41.

In a given season, roughly a third of the points scored are from kickers. That is a really high number! Every time a kicker is on the field, they are expected to score. So unfortunately, any miss is seen as a failure, and as a result, kickers are often undrafted and change teams all the time.

Field goals are most important at the end of the first half and the last quarter. If time is low on the game clock, the time pressure can force a team to try a field goal instead of going for a touchdown, especially if the score is close.

When the margins are that tight, the best way to beat another team is with a field goal. So, kickers are crucial to that success. And if that's the case, wouldn't you want someone who knows what they are doing?

BILL BELICHICK

HEAD COACH

HOMETOWN	NASHVILLE, TENNESSEE
BORN	APRIL 16, 1952
ACTIVE YEARS	1991–1995 AND 2000–PRESENT

CAREER STATS

G: 433

W: 290

L: 143

WIN %: 67

PLAYOFF G: 44

PLAYOFF W: 31

PLAYOFF WIN %: 70.5

6X SUPER BOWL CHAMPION

3X COACH OF THE YEAR
(2003, 2007, AND 2010)

NFL 100TH ANNIVERSARY ALL-TIME TEAM

". . . I'd say really the most important thing for us is to look at future decisions and try to make the best ones that we can."

AT A CROSSROADS

In 1995, Bill Belichick might have been wondering if his career as a head coach was over for good. He had just been fired by the Cleveland Browns and he wasn't sure what he was going to do next. Until that moment, his career had been moving up.

In five seasons, he won thirty-six games and lost forty-four. The Browns only had one winning season in his time there, and that was not good enough for Cleveland, so he was fired and went back to work as an assistant coach. His old friend, legend Bill Parcells, gave him a spot on his coaching staff for the New England Patriots. When Parcells moved on to the New York Jets as head coach in 1997, Belichick followed.

Back in 1979, Belichick got his first long-term coaching gig with the New York Giants. By 1985, he was a defensive coordinator under Parcells. Together, they won a couple of Super Bowls, and Belichick finally got to the top of the ladder when he was named head coach for the Cleveland Browns in 1991.

A BORN LEADER

Coaching was in Belichick's blood. He grew up in Annapolis, Maryland, where his father was an assistant coach for the Naval Academy. From an early age, he watched his father study game film and learned from him about how to create football plays. He would even tag along to meetings with his father. He became a regular at football practices and was already on his way to being a coach.

FROM CAPTAIN TO COACH

Belichick played football in high school but wasn't good enough to receive attention from the big colleges. He went on to college at Wesleyan University, where he played football and lacrosse. He was the captain of his lacrosse team during his senior year in college. Even though he is known for his contributions to football, his favored sport was lacrosse.

Out of college, he started at the bottom of the ladder in football with the Baltimore Colts, and he spent years serving as an assistant coach.

IN CONTROL

In 1999 Parcells retired and Belichick was supposed to be the next head coach of the Jets. But behind the scenes, the Patriots had also been talking to Belichick about being their next head coach. In one of the strangest series of events in the NFL, one day Belichick was introduced as the Jets new head coach and the next day he turned in his resignation.

The Jets felt Belichick was still under an agreement with them, so the NFL made the Patriots send a first-round pick to the Jets for the rights to Belichick. They wanted him that badly. Even after being fired, Belichick had a reputation that was rock solid.

The Patriots believed in Belichick so deeply that they gave him almost complete control over the team. And because they did, history was made. In 2001, the New England Patriots dynasty was born. From 2001 through 2021, they appeared in nine Super Bowls. They won six of them. They went to the playoffs every year except for three, all due to Bill Belichick (and Tom Brady; they were an unstoppable duo).

If you want to understand Belichick, just look at a press conference in 2014. The Patriots had lost 41–14 in a slow start to the season. The media wanted to discuss Tom Brady and the team's poor game the weekend before. Belichick wanted to discuss the upcoming game against the Cincinnati Bengals. For five straight questions, Belichick simply answered questions about Brady and the past with "We're on to Cincinnati," and nothing more.

He only focused on what he could control and change, not what he couldn't. He wouldn't say anything bad about his players, even though they were not playing their best. He knew it would be a long season, and the team had plenty of time to turn it around. He also knew they needed to focus on winning their next game and not dwell on the game they had lost.

The next week, they beat the Bengals 43–17. Not only that, but the team also went on to win the Super Bowl that year. It was their fourth win under Belichick.

A TRUE DYNASTY

Since Belichick has been coach, there is a saying about doing things "The Patriot Way." People don't always agree on what that means, but it involves doing your job, being unselfish, and focusing on winning. "Do your job" is another saying you might hear around the Foxborough stadium.

Belichick has six Super Bowl wins—more than any other coach. He is third all-time in wins (290), and as long as he keeps coaching, will soon be first. He is tied at nineteen with Don Shula for most seasons in the playoffs, and he's coached over forty playoff games, more than any other coach.

Some coaches have a particular way they line up and play on offense and defense—a scheme they always use. They find players to fill those spots based on things like height, weight, and speed. Belichick doesn't do that. He looks for guys who are smart and versatile and who have a desire to be unselfish, and he makes his offense and defense fit them. If everybody does their job, if everybody puts the team ahead of themselves, then they will fit with Belichick.

He is a master at finding the right kind of players for his team and using them in ways that help them succeed.

He never seems too concerned with what other people think about him, and he doesn't worry what the media says about him. He believes in what he's doing. Even after he was fired, he kept on doing the job. And when he got his chance again, he took what he learned in the past and focused that on the future. The past was for learning. The future was for action.

FAST FACTS

- Bill Belichick's first NFL job at the age of twenty-three with the Baltimore Colts paid him $25 a week! At least we know he wasn't doing it for the money.

- The song "Bounce" from the rock band Bon Jovi was dedicated to Bill Belichick.

- Bill Belichick has the nickname "The Hoodie" because he likes to wear that type of sweatshirt. He often cuts the sleeves off.

Runners-up

VINCE LOMBARDI

Vince Lombardi was the coach of the 1960s. His Green Bay Packers won the first two Super Bowls, plus three other titles before that. The Lombardi sweep was their most famous play. It involved their running back going around the end behind two offensive linemen. The Super Bowl trophy was renamed in his honor after his death, and it is now known to fans as the Lombardi Trophy.

BILL WALSH

Bill Walsh led the San Francisco 49ers to three Super Bowl wins in the 1980s. He changed the NFL game with his West Coast offense, which used short passes that acted like running plays. They would stretch a defense across the field and throw short passes to players who would run to open space once they had the ball. Many of his assistant coaches went on to great success of their own in the NFL.

DON SHULA

Don Shula took two different teams to the Super Bowl, the Baltimore Colts and the Miami Dolphins. In 1972, Shula's Dolphins had the only perfect NFL season by going 17-0 and winning the Super Bowl. He only had two losing seasons out of thirty-three as a head coach in the NFL, and he holds the record for the most career wins, at 328.

Legendary Great

GEORGE HALAS

They called him "Papa Bear," but his real name was George Halas, and he coached and owned the Chicago

Bears. In 1920, he helped co-found what would become the NFL. He is one of the giants of the league, and his impact on the NFL cannot be oversold.

Halas believed in the T formation, which had three running backs behind the quarterback. They used this offense to beat Washington 73–0 in the 1940 Championship Game. It went on to inspire many of the offensive formations that followed, some still used today.

Halas coached his last game in 1967, but he still has the second most wins as an NFL head coach, with 318. He won six titles as a head coach of the Bears and is noted for signing college player Red Grange to a contract that gave the league its first superstar. He coached for forty-three years and only had six losing seasons. He was also responsible for daily practices, studying game film, and putting the games on the radio. It's difficult to name anyone who did more for the NFL than George Halas.

Spotlight

WOMEN COACHING STAFF IN THE NFL

In 2021, twelve women were coaching in the NFL. That was the most the league had ever seen. But Jen Welter was first. In 2015, the Arizona Cardinals hired Welter part-time as an intern to help with linebackers. That same year, Sarah Thomas became the first on-field female official. Kathryn Smith became the first full-time female coach when the Buffalo Bills hired her for special teams in 2016. She was joined by San Francisco 49ers coach Katie Sowers in 2017.

Since then, women have slowly been added to the ranks of assistant coaches. Jennifer King recently became the first Black woman coach on a team for the Washington franchise. Lori Locust and Maral Javadifar became the first female coaches to win a Super Bowl when they coached for the Tampa Bay Buccaneers in the 2020 season. With all these incredible coaches, many people think it is only a matter of time before a woman becomes an NFL head coach.

Jen Welter

THE MOST FAMOUS FOOTBALL STADIUM

Lambeau Field is the home of the Green Bay Packers. It even comes with one of the coolest nicknames ever. Temperatures in Green Bay can get pretty cold during football season, so they call it "The Frozen Tundra."

The stadium hosted one of the most famous games in NFL history. Dubbed the "Ice Bowl," it was a 1967 championship game versus the Dallas Cowboys, played in minus-13-degree weather. Because of the cold weather and the rabid fans at Lambeau, it is one of the most feared places to play for opponents. It also has the Lambeau Leap, which refers to when Packers players jump into the stands during celebrations of big plays.

Opened in 1957, it is named for Curly Lambeau, who founded, played for, and coached the Packers. After some renovations, it now holds just over 81,000 people when it's full. It is the oldest stadium that has been continually used by a team in the NFL.

CREATE YOUR
OWN LINEUP

	QB
	RB
	FB
	WR
	TE

	O
	D
	LB
	CB
	S
	K
	COACH

REFERENCES

QUARTERBACK

Gaines, Cork. "6 Quarterbacks Were Picked Before Tom Brady in the 2000 NFL Draft." Yahoo! Sports. February 1, 2022. sports.yahoo.com /6-quarterbacks-were-picked-tom-161136026.html.

Grant, William F. "From $5.50 an Hour to NFL Phenom—The Kurt Warner Story." *The Fordham Ram*. December 1, 2021. thefordhamram.com/83578 /sports/from-5-50-an-hour-to-nfl-phenom-the-kurt-warner-story.

Healy, John. "From Elway to Brady, Ranking the 10 Greatest NFL Quarterbacks of All Time." Audacy, Inc. January 29, 2022. audacy.com /sports/nfl/gallery/best-nfl-quarterbacks-ever#3--joe-montana -ckraz8vgr003f3g6zj6cyf8b.

RUNNING BACK

Biography.com Editors. "Jim Thorpe Biography." A&E Television Networks. Last updated October 14, 2020. biography.com/athlete/jim-thorpe.

———. "Walter Payton Biography." A&E Television Networks. Last updated April 15, 2021. biography.com/athlete/walter-payton.

Fox Sports. "Remembering a Legend: The Life of Walter Payton." FoxSports.com. June 30, 2017. foxsports.com/stories/nfl/remembering-a -legend-the-life-of-walter-payton.

Klein, Christopher. "How Jim Thorpe Became America's First Multi-Sport Star." A&E Television Networks. November 17, 2021. history.com/news /jim-thorpe-sports-native-american-athlete-olympics.

Norris, Luke. "Walter Payton Had His Own 'Flu Game' and Broke an NFL Record Previously Held by O. J. Simpson." Endgame360 Inc. July 4, 2020. sportscasting.com/walter-payton-had-his-own-flu-game-and -broke-an-nfl-record-previously-held-by-o-j-simpson.

Rank, Adam. "Why Bears legend Walter Payton is greatest NFL player of all time." NFL.com. November 21, 2019. nfl.com/news/why-bears -legend-walter-payton-is-greatest-nfl-player-of-all-ti-0ap3000001079212.

Sports Illustrated Staff. "Running Payton's Hill." *Sports Illustrated*. January 31, 2016. si.com/nfl/2016/01/31/themmqb-walter-payton-hill-chicago -bears-nfl.

FULLBACK

Brown, Jim. "How I Play Fullback." *Sports Illustrated*. September 26, 1960. vault.si.com/vault/1960/09/26/how-i-play-fullback.

Donahue, Ben. "Jim Brown: How He Became an NFL Legend (Complete Story)." BrownsNation.com. June 8, 2021. brownsnation.com/jim-brown.

Gosselin, Rick. "State Your Case: Mike Alstott, the Game's Last True Fullback." FanNation. December 15, 2020. si.com/nfl/talkoffame /state-your-case/state-your-case-mike-alstott-the-games-last-true -fullback.

Gribble, Andrew. "58 Years Ago Today: Jim Brown Rushes for NFL Record 237 Yards." ClevelandBrowns.com. November 24, 2015. clevelandbrowns .com/news/58-years-ago-today-jim-brown-rushes-for-nfl-record-237 -yards-16362366.

Judge, Clark. "Why Hall-of-Famer Jim Brown has no equal when it comes to respect from his peers." FanNation. January 15, 2021. si.com/nfl /talkoffame/nfl/jim-brown-and-hall-of-fame.

Maclean, Kevin H. "Jim Brown: The Undisputed Greatest." BleacherReport .com. April 17, 2009. bleacherreport.com/articles/157718-the-undisputed -greatest-jim-brown.

Schwartz, Larry. "SportsCentury Biography: Jim Brown Was Hard to Bring Down." ESPN.com. Accessed March 3, 2022. espn.com/classic /biography/s/Brown_Jim.html.

WIDE RECEIVER

Fitzsimmons, Brian. "Jerry Rice Shared a Story about His Work Ethic—and It's No Wonder He's the GOAT." AOL Sports. September 15, 2015. aol.com/news/2015-09-15-jerry-rice-story-about-how-he-got-his-work -ethic-is-awesome-21236395.html.

Garcia IV, Bob. "Jerry Rice Started Playing Football After Running from High School Principal." Endgame360 Inc. May 17, 2020. sportscasting .com/jerry-rice-started-playing-football-after-running-from-high -school-principal.

———. "Jerry Rice Learned How to Catch by Snagging Bricks." Endgame360 Inc. May 8, 2020. sportscasting.com/jerry-rice-learned-how-to-catch-by -snagging-bricks.

Kerr, Jeff. "Larry Fitzgerald Won't Retire from NFL Yet, But Admits He Won't Return: 'I Had a Great Run.'" CBS Sports. February 16, 2022. cbssports.com/nfl/news/larry-fitzgerald-wont-retire-from-nfl-yet-but -admits-he-wont-return-i-had-a-great-run.

McCauley, Janie. "NFL Legend Jerry Rice Hopes to Catch on as Pro Golfer." *The Seattle Times*. Last updated April 14, 2010. seattletimes.com /sports/golf/nfl-legend-jerry-rice-hopes-to-catch-on-as-pro-golfer-golf.

TIGHT END

Cohen, Rich. "Mike Ditka's Kick-Ass Coaching Tree." *Sports Illustrated*. December 24, 2015. si.com/nfl/2015/12/24/mike-ditka-coaching-tree-ron -rivera-jeff-fisher.

Dixon, John. "Tony Gonzalez—The Kid Who Just Wanted to Have Fun—Is Now in the Hall of Fame." SBNation. August 3, 2019. arrowheadpride .com/2019/8/3/20752753/tony-gonzalez-the-kid-who-just-wanted-to -have-fun-is-now-in-the-hall-of-fame.

Geiser, Bradley. "Pre-NFL Tony Gonzalez Was Better at Basketball Than Football After Playing with a Young Stephon Marbury." Endgame360 Inc. November 12, 2020. sportscasting.com/forget-football -tony-gonzalez-was-better-at-basketball-after-playing-with-future-nba -all-star-stephon-marbury.

Katzowitz, Josh. "After 16 Years, Tony Gonzalez Finally Scores Playoff Win." CBS Sports. January 13, 2013. cbssports.com/nfl/news/after-16 -years-tony-gonzalez-finally-scores-playoff-win.

People for the Ethical Treatment of Animals. "PETA Welcomes Tony Gonzalez to Hall of Fame." PETA.org. Accessed March 15, 2022. peta.org /features/tony-gonzalez-peta-hall-of-fame.

OFFENSIVE TACKLE

Around the NFL Staff. "Paul Brown, Anthony Muñoz Headline Inaugural Class of Bengals Ring of Honor." NFL.com. April 8, 2021. nfl.com/news /paul-brown-anthony-munoz-bengals-ring-of-honor-inaugural-class.

Bendetson, William. "10 Minutes with Former Bengals Offensive Tackle Anthony Muñoz." ESPN.com. October 5, 2007. espn.com/espn /hispanicheritage2007/news/story?id=3047707.

Burke, Chris. "Best of the Firsts, No. 3: Anthony Muñoz." *Sports Illustrated*. April 3, 2012. si.com/nfl/2012/04/03/best-of-the-firsts-no-3-anthony -munoz.

Harvey, Coley. "Bengals' Best Draft Pick is Their Only Hall of Famer, Anthony Muñoz." ESPN.com. April 27, 2016. espn.com/blog /cincinnati-bengals/post/_/id/22405/anthony-munoz-bengals-nfl -draft-best-pick-only-hall-of-famer.

Hobson, Geoff. "20 Years Later, Muñoz Emerging as Hall Giant." The Cincinnati Bengals. August 3, 2018. bengals.com/news/20-years-later -munoz-emerging-as-hall-giant.

Kaufman, Joey. "Anthony Muñoz's Return Sparked USC's 1980 Rose Bowl Victory over Ohio State." *Los Angeles Daily News*. Last updated December 27, 2017. dailynews.com/2017/12/27/anthony-munozs -return-sparked-uscs-1980-rose-bowl-victory-over-ohio-state.

Lamarre, Tom. "A Living Raider Legend, 'Mr. Raider,' Jim Otto." FanNation. February 28, 2021. si.com/nfl/raiders/the-black-hole-plus/jim-otto-pro -football-hall-of-fame-nfl-afl-oakland-raiders-gene-upshaw-art-shell.

Newhan, Ross. "His Faith Produced Miracles: Muñoz Needed It to Come Back and Excel in the NFL." *Los Angeles Times*. November 13, 1985. latimes.com/archives/la-xpm-1985-11-13-sp-5324-story.html.

DEFENSIVE END

Didinger, Ray. "34 Years Ago, the NFL Was Introduced to Reggie White." September 29, 2019. Philadelphia Eagles. philadelphiaeagles.com/news /didinger-34-years-ago-the-nfl-was-introduced-to-reggie-white.

Geiser, Bradley. "Where Are the Vikings' Purple People Eaters Now?" Endgame360 Inc. September 13, 2020. sportscasting.com/where-are -the-vikings-purple-people-eaters-now.

Judge, Clark. "How Did NFL Free Agency Begin? With Reggie White and the Sound of a Gavel." FanNation. March 20, 2021. si.com/nfl /talkoffame/nfl/nfl-free-agency-in-1993.

Klemko, Robert. "How Reggie White Made Green Bay Cool." *Sports Illustrated*. December 6, 2016. si.com/nfl/2016/12/06/nfl-reggie-white-green-bay-black-players-free-agency-history.

Molinaro, Bob. "Bruce Smith Marvels at How Deacon Jones Could Play." *The Virginian-Pilot*. June 4, 2013. pilotonline.com/sports/columns/bob-molinaro/article_d6890edb-9690-5ce1-8528-97574887e10a.html.

LINEBACKER

Center, Bill. "Prototype Butkus Still No. 1 among NFL Linebackers." *The San Diego Union-Tribune*. January 12, 2013. sandiegouniontribune.com/sdut-prototype-butkus-still-no-1-among-nfl-linebackers-2013jan12-story.html.

Dedaj, Paulina. "Steelers Hall of Famer Jack Lambert Auctioning Off Teeth Holder." Fox Sports. March 2, 2021. foxnews.com/sports/steelers-jack-lambert-auctioning-teeth-holder.

DeMarco, David. "Do You Remember the Ferocious Dick Butkus?" WVFN. Last updated May 27, 2020. thegame730am.com/dick-butkus.

Fiammetta, Mike. "Eagles Hall of Famer Chuck Bednarik Dies at 89." *Sports Illustrated*. March 21, 2015. si.com/nfl/2015/03/21/chuck-bednarik-death-philadelphia-eagles#gid=ci0255855030062511&pid=chuck-bednarik.

Jenkins, Dan. "A Special Kind of Brute with a Love of Violence." *Sports Illustrated*. October 12, 1964. vault.si.com/vault/1964/10/12/a-special-kind-of-brute-with-a-love-of-violence.

Thomas, Mike. "Derrick Thomas and the Tragedy That Took a Legend's Life Too Soon." Endgame360 Inc. April 12, 2020. sportscasting.com/derrick-thomas-and-the-tragedy-that-took-a-legends-life-too-soon.

CORNERBACK

Amaranthus, Bri. "Comedy Competition: What's Deion's Next Prime-Time Venture?" FanNation. February 11, 2022. si.com/nfl/cowboys/news/deion-sanders-prime-time-bucket-list-stand-up-comedy-dallas.

Bertha, Mike. "Today in Postseason History: Deion Plays for Falcons, Flies to Pittsburgh for NLCS." MLB Advanced Media. October 11, 2015. mlb.com/cut4/deion-sanders-flies-to-pittsburgh-for-1992-nlcs/c-153956568.

Daley, Bill. "Deion Sanders Has Historic Day." United Press International. October 11, 1992. upi.com/Archives/1992/10/11/Deion-Sanders-has -historic-day/2846718776000.

Lattimore-Volkmann, Laurie. "Don't Forget How Amazing Champ Bailey Was as the True 'Shutdown Corner'." SB Nation. January 24, 2019. milehighreport.com/horse_tracks/2019/1/24/18195290/champ-bailey -pro-football-hall-of-fame-denver-broncos-shutdown-corner-2019.

SAFETY

New York Giants. "Giants Chronicles: Inside Emlen Tunnell's Journey to Becoming a Giants Legend." Accessed March 24, 2022. giants.com/video /inside-emlen-tunnell-s-journey-to-becoming-a-giants-legend.

Pinak, Patrick. "Ronnie Lott Chopped His Pinky Off So He Didn't Miss a Game." FanBuzz. October 8, 2021. fanbuzz.com/nfl/ronnie-lott-pinky.

Salomone, Dan. "Black History Month Tribute: Emlen Tunnell's Giant Legacy." New York Giants. February 1, 2022. giants.com/news/black -history-month-tribute-emlen-tunnell-s-giant-legacy.

KICKER

Dodd, Brian. "4 Leadership Lessons from Justin Tucker's Record Breaking 66-Yard Game-Winning Field Goal." September 27, 2021. briandoddonleadership.com/2021/09/27/4-leadership-lessons-from -justin-tuckers-record-breaking-66-yard-game-winning-field-goal.

Hensley, Jamison. "Justin Tucker's All-Pro Kicking Rooted in Determination—and a Backyard Tree." ESPN.com. November 18, 2017. espn.com/blog/baltimore-ravens/post/_/id/40612/justin-tuckers-all -pro-kicking-rooted-in-determination-and-a-backyard-tree.

Meaney, Mackenzie. "A Year After Making History in College Football, Sarah Fuller is Back Doing What She Loves Most." Sports Illustrated. November 25, 2021. si.com/college/2021/11/25/sarah-fuller-vanderbilt -kicker-reflects-history.

Mink, Ryan. "Justin Tucker Explains How He Hit His Record-Setting Game-Winner." Baltimore Ravens. September 26, 2021. baltimoreravens .com/news/justin-tucker-reacts-to-his-record-setting-game-winner.

———. "10 Questions with Justin Tucker." Baltimore Ravens. September 27, 2018. baltimoreravens.com/news/10-questions-with-justin-tucker.

REFERENCES

Raineri, Joe. "First Woman to Play in College Football Game, at Willamette University, Reflects on Her Experience." KGW-TV. November 30, 2020. kgw.com/article/sports/first-woman-to-play-in-college-football-game -at-willamette-university-reflects-on-her-experience/283-3cb9b758 -3eb2-4839-b1b6-6037652fef2f.

Reichel, Bethany. "Female Kicker Makes NCAA College Football History: The Scholarship Offer." Accessed March 30, 2022. newarena.com /inspirational/female-kicker-makes-ncaa-college-football-history/21.

Solak, Ben. "Justin Tucker's Record-Breaking Field Goal Was a Thing of Destiny." *The Ringer*. September 26, 2021. theringer.com/nfl/2021/9 /26/22695282/justin-tucker-66-yard-field-goal-baltimore-ravens -detroit-lions.

Wells, Mike. "Kicker Adam Vinatieri, NFL's All-Time Leading Scorer, Retiring after 24 Seasons." ESPN.com. May 26, 2021. espn.com /nfl/story/_/id/31515894/adam-vinatieri-nfl-all-leading-scorer-retiring -24-nfl-seasons.

Wertheim, Jon. "Q&A: Examining the Highs, Lows and Doinks of the Current State of NFL Kicking." *Sports Illustrated*. January 7, 2022. si.com /nfl/2022/01/08/q-a-justin-tucker-john-harbaugh-state-of-nfl-kicking.

Zwerneman, Brent. "Reflections on a Rivalry: 10 Years Since Justin Tucker's Kick, but a Texas-A&M Reunion Coming Soon." *Houston Chronicle*. November 24, 2021. houstonchronicle.com/texas-sports-nation/college /article/It-s-been-10-years-since-Justin-Tucker-s-kick-16649905.php.

HEAD COACH

Banks, Don. "Kathryn Smith, the NFL's First Female Full-Time Coach, is Not Thinking about History." *Sports Illustrated*. August 25, 2016. si.com /nfl/2016/08/25/buffalo-bills-kathryn-smith-nfl-assistant-coach.

Brassil, Gillian R. and Kevin Draper. "These Women Were N.F.L. 'Firsts.' They're Eager for Company." *The New York Times*. Last updated February 8, 2021. nytimes.com/2021/02/03/sports/football/nfl-women -coaches.html.

Dussault, Mike. "Cutting Off the Sleeves: The History of Bill Belichick and His Hoodie." Bleacher Report. June 13, 2013. bleacherreport.com /articles/1668165-cutting-off-the-sleeves-the-history-of-bill-belichick -and-his-hoodie.

Elkins, Kathleen. "Bill Belichick Got His First Job in the NFL at Age 23—It Paid $25 a Week." CNBC.com. January 31, 2019. cnbc.com/2019/01/31 /bill-belichick-got-his-first-nfl-job-at-23-it-paid-25-dollars-a-week.html.

Kern, Mason. "Jen Welter and the Backstory on the NFL's Female Coach Pioneer." FanNation. May 19, 2020. si.com/nfl/cardinals/news/jen-welter -coaching-intern-first-female-coach.

Kienzler, Max. "George Halas vs. Vince Lombardi: Who Affected Pro Football More?" Bleacher Report. June 12, 2009. bleacherreport.com /articles/197680-george-halas-vs-vince-lombardi-who-affected- pro-football-more.

Sugrue, Brendan. "Throwback Thursday: George Halas and the Bears Officially Form the NFL." USAToday.com. September 17, 2020. bearswire .usatoday.com/2020/09/17/chicago-bears-throwback-thursday -george-halas-forms-nfl.

STADIUM

Vassalo, Kyle. "The 10 Most Storied Landmarks in NFL History." March 3, 2011. bleacherreport.com/articles/625484-the-10-most-storied-landmarks -in-nfl-history.

INDEX

INDEX

ACKNOWLEDGMENTS

As always, my thanks and love go out to my wife, Jan, who is the best teammate and wife a person could have in this life. Big thanks go out to my mother, Pat, and my brother Steve, as well as my father, Ed, and my brother Mark. Nothing would have been possible without you guys. I would also like to thank and send love to my extended family: Allison, Mike, Violet, Rosie, Audrey, Alex, Della, Milly, Asher, Mary Lou, Scotty, and Trish. Also, Cathy, Marissa, Brenna, Tammy, and Chris—you guys are the best, and I'm lucky to have you. Thanks to Matt Buonaguro for getting me into the book-writing game and Julia Maguire for editing my words into a coherent form.

ABOUT THE AUTHOR

 **DAVID HALPRIN** has been covering American football for the last fifteen-plus years at SB Nation. He is a graduate of Georgia Tech and proudly supports those teams, even when they're not doing so hot. He is the editor-in-chief at *Blogging The Boys* (BloggingTheBoys .com), a Dallas Cowboys site. His previous book was *The Big Book of College Football Trivia: 700 Questions for NCAA Football Fanatics*. He lives with his wife just outside Atlanta, Georgia.